D1391679

The Complete Mixer and Blender

Other Ward Lock books by Mary Norwak

Complete Freezer Recipes
Cooking for your Freezer
Cooking into Europe (Ed)
Freezer and Fridge Cookery
Kitchen Antiques
Preparing Food for your Freezer
The Complete Home Freezer
The Farmhouse Kitchen

Mary Norwak

The Complete
Mixer and Blender

Ward Lock Limited · London

Acknowledgements

The author and publisher would like to record their sincere thanks to the following people and institutions who have helped to provide the illustrations for this book:

Cadbury-Ty.Phoo Ltd (page 118); The Carnation Milk Bureau (page 104); Mrs Julia Hedgecoe (pages 117, 120, 159 and 160); Kenwood (page 78, below); The Kraft Kitchen (page 119); Magimix (page 25, below); New Zealand Lamb Information Bureau (page 77); Pifco Ltd (page 25, top); Sunbeam Electric Ltd (pages 78, top, and 134).

Additional pictures are the copyright of Marshall Cavendish Ltd:

page 26 (photo: Roger Phillips); page 51 (photo: Alan Duns); page 52, top (photo: Mike Leale); and page 52, below (photo: Bryce Attwell).

© Mary Norwak 1977

First published in Great Britain in 1977
by Ward Lock Limited, 116 Baker Street,
London, W1M 2BB, a member of the Pentos Group
Reprinted 1978

Designed by Grant Gibson
House editor Eleanor-Mary Cadell

Text set in 11/13 pt Photon Baskerville,
printed by photolithography, and
bound in Great Britain at The Pitman Press, Bath

British Library Cataloguing in Publication Data
Norwak, Mary
    The complete mixer and blender.
    1. Blenders (Cookery)   2. Mixers (Cookery)
    I. Title
    641.5'89   TX840.B5

ISBN 0-7063-5534-2

Contents

1   Choosing a Machine   7

2   Basic Machine Technique and Maintenance   11

3   Failures and Remedies   17

4   Soups   20

5   Pâtés   31

6   Main Courses and Salads   40

7   Savoury Sauces and Stuffings   66

8   Puddings, Ices and Sweet Sauces   83

9   Bread, Pastry, Cakes, Biscuits and Icings   106

10   Spreads, Pastes and Dips   135

11   Drinks   145

12   Preserves and Pickles   156

13   Saving Time and Money   166

     Index   172

Tables of Temperatures

Domestic oven temperatures				Sugar boiling temperatures		
	Electric °F	Celsius °C	Gas			
Very cool	225	110	$\frac{1}{4}$	Soft ball	237°F	114°C
Very cool	250	130	$\frac{1}{2}$	Hard ball	247°F	119°C
Very cool	275	140	1	Soft crack	280°F	140°C
Cool	300	150	2	Hard crack	310°F	154°C
Warm	325	170	3	Caramel	340°F	171°C
Moderate	350	180	4			
Fairly hot	375	190	5			
Fairly hot	400	200	6			
Hot	425	220	7			
Very hot	450	230	8			
Very hot	475	240	9			

Deep fat frying temperatures

Food	Bread browns in	Fat temperature	Oil temperature
Raw starchy foods doughnuts, fritters, chips (1st frying)	1¼ minutes	325–340°F 170°C	340°F 170°C
Fish in batter	1¼ minutes	325°–340°F 170°C	340°F 170°C
Fish in egg and crumbs	1 minute	360°F 185°C	360°F 185°C
Scotch eggs	1 minute	350°F 180°C	350°F 180°C
Reheated foods potato straws, chips (2nd frying)	40 seconds	380°F 190°C	390°F 195°C

All the spoons referred to in this book are 5ml teaspoons and 15ml tablespoons. They are measured with the contents levelled off, i.e. all the spoons are level spoonsful.

Note
Recipes are for 4–6 servings, according to appetite, except where indicated as in the case of single-serving drinks.
Bulk cooking may be successfully accomplished with mixers and blenders, but the machines must not be overloaded. It is therefore wise to make up the recipe two or three times at one session rather than trying to prepare double or treble quantities in the machine.

1 Choosing a Machine

A mixer, blender or all-in-one food processor with optional attachments can take the place of a team of cooks. Kitchen tasks such as mincing, chopping, crumbing and creaming become a matter of seconds' work rather than occupying endless arduous hours, and this means that more interesting and complicated recipes can be achieved without worry. These machines also represent a significant saving in money as well as time. Larger batches of food can be processed for freezing or turning into jams or pickles, while leftovers can be transformed into delicious meals, and such oddments as stale bread or ends of cheese can be quickly prepared and will save many pence.

Special recipes are not necessary, but preparation methods and timing do differ from traditional hand-mixing techniques. The recipes in this book will give successful results and, after a little practice, favourite recipes can be adapted to the same techniques outlined here. The blender in particular cuts out much preliminary work in recipes, and can help to cut down actual cooking times as well in, for instance, the preparation of flour-based sauces.

The larger machines naturally have a wider variety of uses, but when correctly used small machines can also save considerable time, labour and money. The choice of machine naturally depends on price and possible use, as well as the likely space in a kitchen. It may for instance be convenient in a spacious kitchen to have a large mixer with attachments, a food processor, or a kitchen centre (see page 9), but a smaller kitchen might be better served by a free-standing blender and a hand-held electric mixer, which can be stored easily in a drawer. A single person or small family would be happy with this combination for the making of occasional cakes, for whipping cream or mashing potatoes, preparing individual drinks, and grinding enough coffee for breakfast. A larger family with children might find a large mixer/blender in constant use for batches of cakes and pastry, puddings and main dishes, and the preparation of drinks and soups. They might also appreciate a mincer attachment to deal with large quantities of raw or cooked meat, or a slicer and shredder for salad preparation. The really keen cook would appreciate a cream-making attachment, juice extractor, or colander-and-sieve for preparing food for the freezer, and needs a powerful blender for making breadcrumbs, chopping nuts or chocolate.

The range of machines is wide, so try to study leaflets and see models demonstrated before making a final choice:

A large mixer with a stand and bowl is often available with a variety of attachments. It is strong enough to tackle up to quite large quantities, provided they are added in small amounts. These machines are heavy and must be kept permanently in a convenient place, to be used at the turn of a switch.

A small mixer may be with or without a stand and bowl. It is less powerful and must not be overstrained, so it should not be used for heavy mixtures or large quantities. Some small mixers are attached to their stands; others can be detached and used as hand-held mixers. A hand-held mixer is often a useful supplement to a larger one for a busy cook, for whipping cream or egg whites. Hand-held mixers are mainly designed for whisking, but can also be used for light creaming and 'rubbing-in'. Care must be taken not to overstrain the motor with heavy work. Some of these mixers have only a single speed. Others, however, have variable speeds to suit the work involved.

A small blender may be free-standing or an attachment. It is useful for all blending jobs, especially really fine chopping and grinding. Some free-standing models have special grinder attachments for this work. This type of blender should be run for a few seconds only at a time to avoid overheating, and it should not be used for very stiff mixtures. Food can only be blended in small quantities, so soups and drinks may be laborious and messy to make. More liquid may be needed in more powerful blenders, and this may limit one in making highly spiced mixtures.

A large blender may also be either free-standing or an attachment to a mixer. It normally has a working capacity of $1\frac{1}{2}$ pints/750ml or over. This type of blender can tackle all kinds of blending jobs, and can often be used for chopping or grinding.

A wide-based blender is powerful and not suitable for small quantities of ingredients or for fine chopping; it purées them too soon. However, this type is particularly good for large amounts of drinks or soups, and can also be used for such jobs as rubbing fat into flour.

A kitchen centre (Sunbeam) has a powerful motor base similar to a free-standing blender and is controlled by a press-button panel. The base can be fitted with a blender, mixer or mincer to tackle a wide range of jobs.

A food processor (Magimix) has a powerful motor base fitted with a cylindrical container and a variety of knives and shredding discs. Jobs are done according to the knife or shredder which is attached, and the motor is controlled by movement of the bowl, so only one speed is used.

Attachments

Additional attachments that can be speedily fitted to large mixers are available. They do many specialized jobs and are very useful when large quantities of food have to be prepared, or if certain routine tasks occur frequently, such as the extraction of fruit juice or the preparation of yeast doughs. Full instructions for fitting and use are given with each attachment, but a brief indication of their various uses will enable a mixer-owner to ascertain if they are necessary. In fact, so many jobs, such as grinding coffee or preparing fruit purée can be accomplished by the blender, that the intelligent use of just mixer and blender will be adequate for the normal needs of most households.

Mincer and sausage filler
The mincer has both fine and large-hole mincing screens, so that mixtures may be cut finely for pies and pâtés, or coarsely for sausages or animal food. The mincer includes a pestle for pushing food down into the machine, which can deal speedily with large quantities of meat, fish and vegetables. An inexpensive sausage filler can be fitted to the mincer to enable the minced meat to be fed into sausage skins.

Slicer and shredder
This attachment consists of four 'drums', which produce slices or shreds of such foods as root vegetables, apples, cabbages, onions, potatoes, cheese, suet, nuts, chocolate and cucumber. It is useful for anyone who makes large quantities of salads.

Colander and sieve
This attachment is useful for preparing purées and baby foods. While a blender will purée cooked or raw ingredients, it is necessary to sieve such items as gooseberries and currants to remove the pips.

The colander and sieve are also useful for converting quantities of garden produce for bottling or home freezing.

Coffee mill
This attachment grinds coffee beans to the degree required from coarse to fine. Many people will find a blender adequate to grind coffee.

Bean slicer and pea huller
The bean-slicing attachment can also be converted to use for shelling peas. This is a useful machine if a large quantity of garden produce is to be processed for home freezing.

Juice extractor
This attachment extracts all juice from oranges, lemons or grapefruit. It is very useful for mothers of small children. With the addition of an *oil dripper*, it can be used to make mayonnaise, although this can be made equally well by the mixer beaters or blender.

Juice separator
This attachment is used to extract juice from fruit or vegetables, straining it at the same time, and will tackle 1lb/400g of fruit or vegetables at a time. It consists of a drum container fitted with a plastic filter and straining basket which is attached to the high-speed outlet of a mixer.

Can opener
This attachment opens any shape of can speedily and efficiently, with no danger of cut fingers. A magnet lifts the lid clear.

Potato peeler
This attachment can be used to peel any root vegetable very cleanly, and is useful for large families.

Dough hook
This hook is used for kneading yeast, doughs, and makes light work of this rather heavy task. As this is a very inexpensive attachment, it is well worth buying for anyone who likes to make bread or yeast cakes.

Cream maker
This attachment is used to make thick or pouring cream from un-salted butter and warm milk, and it can also be used for ice-cream preparation.

2 Basic Machine Technique and Maintenance

It is most important that all machines are kept on a working surface where they can be used regularly as part of kitchen routine. If they are put away in cupboards, or high on shelves, it will be an effort to make use of a mixer, blender or attachment, and their potential for saving time and energy will be minimized. If the machine is ready set up, it can be used dozens of times in the course of a cooking session, quickly washed and reassembled and the cook will speed up her routine and produce far more and far better dishes.

Never place a machine on a wet surface, nor allow a motor to get wet. Keep them clean and away from excess heat. Machines should be wiped over with a damp cloth and polished with a dry one, but never cleaned with an abrasive material, nor immersed in water. Never let food particles accumulate on parts of the machine; it is best to wipe over the underside of beaters with a damp cloth after each use, as dry powders in particular can quickly coat the surface.

To wash a mixer beater, bowl, blender goblet or attachment, put into warm soapy water, rinse and dry thoroughly. If food particles are lodged under the blades of a blender, put some warm water and liquid detergent into the blender goblet and run the machine for a few seconds before rinsing and drying. All metal parts of a machine or its attachments should be washed in warm soapy water (not washing soda), then dried well before storage. All plastic parts should be wiped over with hot soapy water and well dried, but not exposed to direct heat such as a cooker or oven. Wash glass parts with hot soapy water, but do not expose them to sudden changes of temperature.

Attachments used for preparing fruit, vegetables or fruits which stain should also be washed straight after use. These must be dried very carefully, and stored loosely assembled so that air can circulate. For convenience, they can be stored in a wire vegetable rack so that the heads rest on the wire lattice and the rods go through the holes.

This makes the attachments easy to see, and cutting edges cannot be damaged.

To avoid damage to machines, it is important not to overstrain them with over-heavy mixtures or long running times. Long continuous running can damage machines, and generally a mixer should not run for more than 3 minutes at a time, nor a blender for more than 45–60 seconds. It is best to process small quantities of food at a time, and to switch on and off once or twice during working time. Often, it is necessary to scrape down food in mixing bowls or blender goblets. This should never be done while the motor is running, and sharp implements such as knives or spoons should not be used; most machines are supplied with a suitable spatula.

Basic mixer technique

Hand-made recipes can be used for an electric mixer without difficulty, but it is very easy to work the machine too quickly or for too long and an over-beaten mixture will spoil results. Start mixtures on slow speed, and increase speed as required, but don't leave the machine to work away on its own without constant checks to see that the mixture is not being overworked. Some mixers have planetary action with the beaters turning and revolving on axis, so that the mixture comes cleanly from the sides of the bowl, and mixing is more thorough and smoother. Ordinary beaters force the mixture outwards so that it clings to the sides of the mixing bowl. If the mixture adheres to the sides of the bowl, stop the machine and scrape down the sides with a spatula or wooden spoon before starting the motor again. For the best results, ingredients should be at room temperature, as mixing will take longer if the ingredients are cold.

Running speeds (mixer)

The correct speed for a mixer can be judged by the work to be done and the quantity of ingredients involved. Basically, a heavy mixture needs slow beating, and over-beating will result in heavy cakes, grainy cream and curdled eggs. For a light mixture, a higher speed is needed.

Use a *low speed* for rubbing in pastry and cakes, *medium speed* for creaming mixtures, and *high speed* for whisking egg whites. The heavy beater of a large mixer is generally used for cake mixtures and the whisk for light egg whites or very light mixtures. When a mixer has a variety of speeds, the speed may be altered during processing. Often a recipe recommends starting on a low speed, and then increasing speed for final mixing once the ingredients have been incorporated.

Creaming butter and sugar

Begin on minimum speed and increase to speed 2 when fat and sugar have been bound together.

Beating in eggs

Add eggs one at a time at speed 2, and beat until the mixture is like whipped cream.

Folding in flour and fruit

Reduce speed to minimum, tip in all the flour, then fruit and liquid, and switch off as soon as they are mixed in.

Rubbing fat into flour

Cut the fat into pieces, put in bowl and switch to minimum speed, then tip in the flour. When fat has broken down a little, increase to speed 2. When mixture is like fine breadcrumbs, add water for pastry and switch off as soon as it is mixed in.

Biscuit doughs

Mix on speed 2.

Mashed potatoes

Start at minimum speed and increase to speed 2.

Royal icing and marzipan

Mix on minimum speed.

Quantities (mixer)

While the mixer is useful for making two cakes at a time and saving a lot of effort, it is important not to over-fill the mixer bowl. Recommended quantities for a large mixer are:

Egg whites

10–12 ($\frac{1}{2}$ pint/250ml) maximum; 1 egg white minimum.

Cake or pudding mixture

6lb/3kg all ingredients maximum; 2oz/50g butter with 2oz/50g sugar minimum.

Pastry

1$\frac{1}{2}$lb/600g flour and 12oz/300g fat maximum; 4oz/100g flour and 2oz/50g fat minimum.

Yeast dough

2lb/1kg flour and proportionate ingredients.

Basic blender technique

A blender cuts down considerably on work in the kitchen, since it can be used for chopping cooked meat and fish, chopping vegetables, making breadcrumbs, grinding nuts and chopping herbs. In addition, it is useful for smoothing sauces, soups, drinks and purées, and for preparing batters, mousses and diet foods. One or two machines can also be used for chopping raw flesh, which saves considerable time in preparing pâtés and other meat recipes. As with mixers, it is important not to over-process ingredients and to time processing carefully at the correct speed for the job.

A blender works by forming a vortex or 'hole' in the mixture. Briefly, the mixture to be blended is pushed up the sides of the goblet and then falls down into the centre and on to the blades. To prevent the blender labouring too hard, start with a small amount of the liquid used in the recipe. Cut fruit, vegetables and meat into small cubes, and break bread or biscuits into small chunks. Remove any fruit stones, or pieces of bones from meat before blending. Use a low speed for chopping and for coarse textures, and start at a low speed increasing to high when larger quantities of food are being blended (over half a goblet full). Work in only small quantities of heavy mixture at a time, and switch quickly 'off' then 'on' to low or high speed to push the food down on to the blades. If food gets lodged under the blades, stop the machine and scrape the blades with a rubber or plastic spatula or wooden spoon. Scrape or push the food down from time to time, but don't do this while the motor is running.

It is important never to over-fill the goblet, and to cover it before blending. Hold the lid lightly in place with one hand when starting the motor. The lid should not be taken off during use, unless extra ingredients have to be added while the machine is running, but this is best done by removing the central knob in the lid.

A blender motor is dangerously powerful, and children should be kept away from the blender when it is in use. See that nobody puts fingers, hands or implements into the goblet while the motor is running. Don't leave the blender plugged in when not in use, and do see that it is always firmly attached to the base when running, and standing firmly on a level surface.

When using a blender recipe, add the ingredients to the goblet in the order given. If you are adapting a normal recipe, try to adapt to blender technique by blending liquids or soft ingredients first, adding ingredients to be chopped or ground after the first blending. See that fats and eggs are at room temperature, or melt the fat before blending. Liquids may be warmed before adding to ease blending, but hot liquids should not be put in the goblet. Be careful not to overblend, which will spoil the texture of food. Time the blending, using correct speeds, and watch the consistency of food being blended. When chopping such items as nuts, only process a small quantity at a time, or the nuts lower in the goblet will be ground to a fine powder by the time the nuts above are chopped. Follow manufacturers' instructions very carefully if grinding hard substances such as coffee beans, chocolate or nuts, or if preparing raw meat or fish.

A blender is a useful maid-of-all-work, but there are one or two jobs better handled by other tools. A blender cannot be used for beating egg whites or for crushing whole ice cubes (cubes have to be broken into small pieces before adding to liquids in the blender). The blender cannot be used for mashing potatoes, processing large quantities of cooked meat, or mincing raw meat, and it will not slice or shave nuts. The blender can be used for making batters for cake mixture, and for quick creaming of fat, eggs and sugar, but it is not suitable for making a complete cake mixture, which is better finished off with a mixer beater. The blender cannot be used for mixing light sponge cakes.

Running speeds (blender)

Some blenders have a marked dial, or a series of buttons, either marked 'off', 'low' and 'high', or with a set of numbers. High speed or a high number is for liquid mixtures, while low speed or low numbers are for mixing heavier ingredients, or for chopping.

Quantities (blender)

A blender should never be filled more than three-quarters full, and it is wise to divide recipe quantities into small amounts if necessary. Workable blending quantities are:

Liquids
1 pint/500ml to 1½ pints/750ml, according to size of blender

Pastes and spreads
4oz/100g at one time

Bread and biscuit crumbs
2oz/50g at one time

Cooked vegetables for purée
4oz/100g at one time

Soups
1 pint/500ml liquid and 8oz/200g solids

Fruit for purée
2oz/50g at one time, without pips or stones

Dried fruit
2oz/50g at one time

Batter
1 pint/500ml

The Magimix

The Magimix is a food processor that combines the functions of a mixer, blender, slicer and grater, and it can be used for preparing the same recipes as the more traditional mixer and blender with attachments. It has the advantage that it can be used for preparing raw meat and fish, and is particularly valuable for preparing a wide variety of sliced, shredded or chopped vegetables and fruit, grated cheese and breadcrumbs. The Magimix also has a juice extraction attachment.

The machine is of somewhat different construction from other mixer/blenders, consisting of a bowl on a heavy motor base. A series of knives or cutters can be fitted according to use and then a lid put on with a hopper through which food can be pushed with a plastic pusher. The machine is operated by a simple turn of the bowl, which connects to switch on the motor, and it works very quickly indeed, most processes only taking 5 seconds. A very comprehensive booklet is issued with the machine, which should be studied before using the Magimix for recipes in this book.

3 Failures and Remedies

There is an obvious difference between hand and machine techniques, which can create small problems during machine preparation, or poor textured results when the cook first uses a mixer and blender. Experience in use usually overcomes these difficulties, but it is possible to avoid problems right from the beginning. The following points indicate the problems and their remedies.

Mixture sticks to bowl or mixer beater
This indicates that the ingredients are not warm enough. Fat should always be at room temperature before being used. Eggs which have been stored in a refrigerator or very cold place should also be at room temperature before being used.

Mixture climbs too high up sides of mixer bowl
This means that the mixer is being used at too high a speed. The motor should be stopped and the mixture scraped back into the bottom of the bowl before the motor is switched on again at a lower speed.

Small quantity of mixture is not mixed thoroughly
The beater may need closer adjustment to the bowl.

Egg whites are not whisked high and fluffy
This can mean that the eggs are too new, or too cold. It may also indicate that the speed is too slow. It is also important that the bowl and whisk should be completely clean and dry, and free from egg yolk or grease. The whisk should be adjusted as closely as possible, and the maximum speed should be used.

Pastry is 'short' and difficult to roll

This can mean that too much fat has been used, or that it has been over-mixed. A mixer rubs in very thoroughly, so that a little less fat can be used than usual, and the work is done in a very short time. When liquid is added, it should also be put in quickly and the motor turned off as soon as it has been incorporated, or the pastry will be over-mixed.

Pastry is like rubber

Water has been added too slowly and mixed in between additions. Water should be tipped into pastry quickly and the motor switched off at once.

Cake is 'heavy'

This indicates that the flour has been mixed in too vigorously, or for too long. Flour should be folded in at minimum speed, and the machine should be switched off as soon as it is incorporated.

Food is chopped too finely

With a blender, it is very easy to over-chop so that items like nuts are ground finely instead of chopped. Only process small quantities at a time, or the lower nuts will be ground while those at the top are being chopped. Work on minimum speed for a very short time.

Food sticks and is not blended

This indicates that there is not enough liquid in the blender goblet, or that the blender is overloaded. Solid ingredients should be added slowly in small quantities so that blending is smooth and even. If the mixture sticks, stop the motor and scrape down the sides, or remove some of the ingredients and process smaller quantities. In a creamed mixture, the ingredients may be too cold.

Cream curdles

This means that cream has been over-blended. It should be added gradually to blender recipes, and the motor should be switched off as soon as the cream has been mixed in.

Soft cheese packs together

Oil is pressed out from some cheeses during blending, and it is a good idea to put a little flour or bread from the recipe into the blender with the cheese during processing so that it absorbs the oil and enables the cheese to grate evenly.

Cheese sauce curdles

This will happen if the raw cheese is blended with the other raw ingredients before cooking, and it will overcook. Grate the sauce separately and add to the cooked sauce.

Icing is too soft
Ingredients in a blender should be at room temperature, but if they are too warm, blending will thin the mixture. Leave the icing to cool and firm up before using.

4 Soups

Soups make an attractive beginning to a meal, but they are also useful as an almost complete meal if accompanied by fresh crusty bread and butter, a piece of cheese and some fresh fruit. There are three basic ways of making soup with the blender. The raw vegetables may be chopped in the blender and then cooked, which results in a nourishing soup made with the minimum of cooking (the vegetables may also be shredded or thinly sliced with an attachment if this is preferred). For a cream soup, the vegetables may be prepared in this way and blended a second time after cooking, or they may be roughly chopped by hand, cooked and then blended. The third type of soup can be made from leftovers such as cooked vegetables, gravy and meat with additional stock blended together and then thoroughly heated.

When vegetables are cooked before the addition of stock or water, butter or dripping gives the best flavour in the preliminary sealing by heat. A well-flavoured stock is essential for good soup, made from a chicken carcase, giblets, or fresh beef or veal bones. Stock may be prepared in advance and refrigerated or frozen until needed. If stock is not available, flavouring may be given by stock cubes, but it is important to taste carefully before serving, as these cubes are often very salty and it may be necessary to adjust seasoning.

When a soup needs additional thickening, this may be achieved with a little flour, but a better flavour will result from using cooked potato, rice or pasta, vegetable or tomato purée. These may all be blended into the soup to give smoothness. Cream may be specified as a thickener in a recipe, but this should only be blended in at the last minute and the motor turned off as soon as the cream has been blended in, as it curdles if over-blended.

A soup need not necessarily be served hot, and an ice-chilled soup makes a delicious but nourishing complete meal or first course during the summer. Fruit soups are also delicious as a preliminary to a salad meal, but they should not be over-sweetened. All soups benefit from an attractive garnish, such as chopped herbs or crisp bacon, whipped cream or soured cream, or bread cubes either toasted or fried.

Artichoke Soup

1½lb/600g *Jerusalem artichokes*
1 *teaspoon/5ml lemon juice*
1 *small onion*
2oz/50g *butter*
1½ *pints/750ml stock*
½oz/15g *cornflour*
3fl.oz/75ml *single cream*
Salt and pepper

Peel and slice the artichokes and put them into a little water with the lemon juice to prevent discolouration. Peel the onion and chop it coarsely in the blender. Melt the butter and cook the chopped onion gently in it until soft but not brown. Add the artichoke slices and continue cooking for 5 minutes. Put the artichokes, onions and liquid from the cooking into the blender, with the stock. Add the cornflour mixed with a little cold stock. Blend for 1 minute until smooth. Reheat and stir in cream just before serving. Season with salt and pepper to taste. Be careful not to boil the soup when the cream has been added.

Asparagus Soup

1 *small onion*
2oz/50g *butter*
1oz/25g *plain flour*
12oz/300g *cooked or canned asparagus*
1 *pint/500ml chicken stock*
½ *pint/250ml milk*
Salt and pepper

Peel the onion and chop it coarsely in the blender. Melt the butter, and cook the onion until soft but not brown. Work in the flour, and continue cooking, stirring well, for 1 minute. Put the mixture into the blender with the asparagus cut in pieces, add stock and milk. Blend for 1 minute. Simmer gently for 5 minutes, and season to taste with salt and pepper. A few asparagus tips may be reserved for garnish.

Beetroot Soup

12oz/300g *beetroot*
1 *medium onion*
¾ *pint/375ml chicken or beef stock*
3 *celery leaves*
Salt and pepper
1 *teaspoon sugar*
2 *tablespoons/30ml lemon juice*
4fl.oz/100ml *commercial sour cream*
1 *pickled cucumber*

The beetroot may be freshly cooked, bottled or canned. If the beetroot has been preserved in vinegar, rinse it well before using, and check the seasoning carefully, as it may be advisable to use less lemon juice. Cut the beetroot into pieces and put into the blender with the roughly chopped onion, stock, celery leaves, salt, pepper and sugar. Cover and blend until the beetroot is finely chopped. Put into a saucepan and simmer for 10 minutes. Add the lemon juice. Serve hot or cold, topped with sour cream and chopped pickled cucumber.

Celery Soup

10 *sticks celery*
1 *medium onion*
1½ *pints/750ml chicken stock*
1 *teaspoon salt*

Cut the celery into 1in/2.5cm pieces. Peel the onion and cut into pieces. Put celery, onion and stock into the blender, and chop coarsely. It may be necessary to process the vegetables in two or three lots so that the blender is not overloaded. Put into a saucepan with the salt, bring to the boil, and then simmer for 10 minutes. Put into the blender and blend until smooth. Reheat and serve hot with cubes of fried bread. If a cream soup is preferred, use ½ pint/250ml creamy milk instead of part of the stock, and add it at the second blending stage.

Cheese Soup

1 *small onion*
2oz/50g *butter*
2oz/50g *plain flour*
2 *medium carrots*
¾ *pint/375ml chicken stock*
¾ *pint/375ml milk*
4oz/100g *Cheddar cheese*
Salt and pepper

Peel the onion and chop it finely in the blender. Melt the butter and cook the onion until just soft. Work in the flour and cook gently for 1 minute. Cut the carrots into small pieces. Put the carrots, onion mixture, chicken stock and milk into the blender, and blend for 1 minute. Put the blended mixture into a saucepan, and simmer for 5 minutes. Grate the cheese and stir into the soup. Heat gently, add seasoning, and stir until the cheese has melted. Serve hot with a garnish of chopped parsley or chives.

Cream of Corn Soup

1 *medium onion*
1 *large potato*
2oz/50g *butter*
1½ *pints/750ml chicken stock*
12oz/300g *sweetcorn kernels*
¼ *pint/125ml milk*
2 *teaspoons cornflour*
Salt and pepper

The sweetcorn kernels may be canned or frozen. Peel the onion and potato, cut into pieces and put into the blender. Cover and chop coarsely. Melt the butter and cook the onion and potato gently for 5 minutes. Add the stock, bring to the boil and simmer for 15 minutes. Add the sweetcorn kernels, and cook for 5 minutes. Put into the blender, cover and blend for 1 minute. Add the milk and blend for 10 seconds. Mix the cornflour with a little milk or water, pour on the soup, and reheat, stirring well. Season with salt and pepper. The soup is good served with a garnish of chopped parsley, or small toasted bread cubes, or crumbled crisp bacon.

Creamed Fish Soup

1 *small onion*
12oz/300g *white fish*
½ *pint/250ml water*
1oz/25g *butter*
1 *tablespoon parsley*
1oz/25g *plain flour*
½ *pint/250ml milk*
Salt and pepper
2oz/50g *peeled shrimps*

The fish can be a mixture of white fish, and a little smoked haddock may be included. Peel and chop the onion and put into the water with the fish. Simmer until just soft. Put into the blender including the cooking liquid, with the butter, parsley, flour and milk. Blend until smooth. Pour into a saucepan and heat gently, stirring until smooth and hot. Season to taste and garnish with shrimps.

Garden Soup

8oz/200g *leeks*
8oz/200g *carrots*
8oz/200g *celery*
8oz/200g *potatoes*
8oz/200g *onions*
8oz/200g *shelled peas*
2 *garlic cloves*
4oz/100g *butter*
2 *tablespoons/30ml olive oil*
½oz/15g *parsley*
Salt and pepper
Pinch of ground mace
½ *pint/250ml single cream*

If all the vegetables are not available fresh, some frozen ones may be used. Clean the leeks, carrots and celery, and peel the potatoes and onions. Put into the blender with the peas in small quantities and chop coarsely. Crush the garlic cloves and add to the vegetables. Melt the butter in a heavy saucepan, add the vegetables and shake and stir over moderate heat for 5 minutes. Add the oil, chopped parsley and seasoning, with water to cover. Cover and simmer for 2 hours. Return to blender and blend to a purée, and reheat, adding cream just before serving. Sprinkle with a little chopped parsley or chopped cooked bacon if liked.

Kidney Soup

4 *lambs' kidneys*
1 *onion*
1oz/25g *butter*
½oz/15g *plain flour*
1 pint/500ml *water*
¼ pint/125ml *milk*
Salt and pepper
1 *tablespoon/15ml sherry*

Skin the kidneys and remove the cores, and cut the flesh into small pieces. Peel the onion, cut into pieces, and chop in the blender. Melt the butter and cook the onion gently for 3 minutes. Add the kidneys and cook for 5 minutes. Work in the flour, cook for 2 minutes and add the water. Bring to the boil and simmer for 10 minutes. Put into the blender with the milk and blend until smooth. Return to the saucepan, season well with salt and pepper and reheat. Add the sherry just before serving, and garnish with chopped parsley or small cubes of fried or toasted bread.

Leek and Potato Soup

1lb/400g leeks
1lb/400g potatoes
2oz/50g butter
1¼ pints/625ml chicken stock
½ pint/250ml milk
Salt and pepper
Chives

Clean the leeks well and cut the white parts into pieces. Cut the potatoes in pieces. Melt the butter and simmer the vegetables for 5 minutes. Add the stock, cover and simmer for 20 minutes. Put into the blender, cover, and blend for 10 seconds. Add milk, cover, and blend for 5 seconds. Reheat gently, seasoning with salt and pepper, and garnish with chopped chives. This soup can also be served chilled with the addition of a little thin cream and is then usually called *Vichyssoise*.

Lentil Soup

12oz/300g lentils
6 tomatoes
1 onion
3 pints/1.5 litres stock
Salt and pepper
4oz/100g bacon

If possible, use some stock left from cooking a bacon joint, if it is not too salty. Soak the lentils in cold water to cover for 12 hours. Dip the tomatoes in boiling water and skin them. Cut up the tomatoes, removing the seeds. Cut the onion in rings. Put the soaked lentils into the stock with tomatoes and onion and simmer for about 1 hour until soft. Put into the blender, cover, and blend for 10 seconds. Reheat, seasoning to taste, and garnish with crisply fried bacon crumbled into small pieces.

Mushroom Soup

8oz/200g mushrooms
2 pints/1 litre water
1 small onion
2oz/50g butter
1½oz/40g plain flour
¼ pint/125ml milk
Salt
Pinch of nutmeg
¼ pint/125ml thin cream
Chopped fresh parsley

Wipe the mushrooms, but do not peel them. Cut into pieces and put into the blender with half the water. Cover and blend for 5 seconds. Put into a saucepan. Peel the onion, cut into pieces and put into the blender. Cover and blend for 5 seconds. Cook the onion in the butter until glossy, and stir in the flour. Cook until light yellow. Add the mushroom mixture with remaining water and milk and simmer for 10 minutes. Season with salt and a pinch of nutmeg. Just before serving, add the cream and garnish with chopped parsley.

Cream of Onion Soup

2 rashers streaky bacon
8oz/200g onions
1oz/25g butter
½oz/15g flour
1½ pints/750ml milk
Salt and pepper
1½oz/40g grated cheese
Chopped fresh parsley

Cut the bacon in pieces and chop coarsely in the blender. Fry gently to extract the fat. Peel the onions, cut in pieces, and chop finely in the blender. Add the onions to the bacon with the butter and cook slowly until the onions are soft but not coloured. Sprinkle in the flour, mix well and gradually add the milk and seasoning. Bring to the boil and simmer for 10 minutes. Blend until smooth and reheat. Grate the cheese in the blender and put it into a tureen. Pour on the soup, and garnish with a little chopped parsley.

Right: Free-standing
blender by Pifco.

Below: The Magimix food
processor, a maid of all work.

Fresh Pea Soup

1 *small onion*
2*oz/50g butter*
1*lb/400g green peas (shelled weight)*
Pinch of mace
Sprig of parsley
½ *teaspoon salt*
1 *teaspoon sugar*
¾ *pint/375ml water*
½ *pint/250ml creamy milk*
Pepper

If fresh peas are not available, use the equivalent weight of frozen peas, and let them thaw slightly before using. Peel the onion and chop it coarsely in the blender. Melt the butter and cook the onion until soft. Add the peas, mace, parsley, salt, sugar and water and simmer for 20 minutes. Put into the blender, cover and blend for 1 minute. Add milk and blend for 10 seconds. Return to saucepan, reheat gently, and season with pepper and more salt to taste. For garnish, use a little chopped mint, small fried bread cubes, or crumbled crisp bacon.

Split Pea Soup

4*oz/100g split peas*
1 *large onion*
1 *medium carrot*
1 *medium turnip*
1 *bacon rasher*
1*oz/25g butter*
1 *teaspoon sugar*
1½ *pints/750ml stock*
½ *pint/250ml milk*
Salt and pepper

If it is possible to use stock from boiling bacon, this will give the soup a delicious flavour. It may be rather salty though, so check seasoning carefully and do not add any extra salt until the soup is ready to serve. Put the split peas into the blender, cover and blend for 1 minute. Peel the onion, carrot and turnip, and remove rind from the bacon rasher. Cut vegetables and bacon into small pieces. Melt the butter and cook the onion and bacon until golden brown. Add the carrot and turnip and cook for 2 minutes, stirring well. Add the peas, sugar and stock, and simmer for 45 minutes. Pour into the blender, add milk and blend for 1 minute. Return to saucepan and reheat, seasoning with salt and pepper to taste. Garnish with small cubes of fried bread.

Tomato Soup

1 *small onion*
1 *bacon rasher*
1*oz/25g butter or bacon fat*
1*lb/400g ripe tomatoes*
1 *medium potato*
½ *pint/250ml water*
1 *teaspoon salt*
½ *teaspoon sugar*
½ *teaspoon paprika*
½ *teaspoon celery salt*
¼ *teaspoon cayenne pepper*
¼ *pint/125ml milk*

Peel the onion and remove rind from the bacon rasher. Cut the onion and bacon into pieces, and soften in butter or bacon fat until the onion is golden brown. Dip the tomatoes in boiling water and remove skins. Cut in pieces and remove pips. Peel the potato and cut in slices. Add the tomatoes, potato and water to the onion and bacon, cover and simmer for 30 minutes. Put into the blender, add the seasonings, and blend for 1 minute. Add the milk, cover and blend for 10 seconds. Reheat the soup gently and serve with a garnish of a little whipped cream and chopped parsley. If tomatoes are out of season, canned tomatoes can be used. Substitute 1lb/400g can of tomatoes, including the liquid, but sieve the soup after blending to get rid of the pips.

Opposite: Vichyssoise, made by adding cream to the basic Leek and Potato Soup (page 24).

Tomato and Carrot Soup

1 *small onion*
1*oz/25g butter*
1*lb/400g tomatoes*
6*oz/150g carrots*
$\frac{3}{4}$ *pint/375ml water*
1 *teaspoon sugar*
1 *teaspoon salt*
1 *teaspoon celery salt*
Pepper
Chopped fresh parsley

Peel the onion and chop it roughly in the blender. Melt the butter and cook the onion gently for 3 minutes. Dip the tomatoes in boiling water and skin them. Cut in pieces and remove the pips. Cut up carrots roughly. Put tomatoes, carrots, half the water, sugar and seasonings into a saucepan. Bring to the boil, cover and simmer for 10 minutes. Put the remaining water into the blender, add the soup, cover and blend for 30 seconds. Reheat and garnish with a little chopped parsley.

Tomato and Potato Soup

2 *leeks*
1*oz/25g butter*
8*oz/200g tomatoes*
12*oz/300g potatoes*
1$\frac{1}{2}$ *pints/750ml water*
1 *teaspoon salt*
1 *teaspoon sugar*
3*fl.oz/75ml single cream*

Clean the leeks and remove the green parts. Cut up the white pieces and put into the blender. Cover and chop for 10 seconds. Melt the butter and cook the leeks gently until just soft. Dip the tomatoes into boiling water to loosen the skins. Skin the tomatoes and remove the pips. Cut into pieces and put into the blender. Cover and blend for 5 seconds. Add to the leeks and cook gently for 5 minutes. Peel the potatoes, cut in pieces and put into the blender with one third of the water. Blend for 5 seconds. Add to the leek and tomato mixture together with remaining water. Add salt and sugar, cover and simmer for 25 minutes. Pour into the blender, cover and blend for 10 seconds. Reheat, and just before serving, stir in the cream. If liked, garnish with a little chopped fresh parsley or chives, or a little crumbled crisp bacon.

Watercress Soup

1 *bunch watercress*
1*lb/400g potatoes*
1$\frac{1}{2}$ *pints/750ml chicken stock*
$\frac{1}{2}$ *pint/250ml milk*
$\frac{1}{2}$*oz/15g cornflour*
Salt and pepper

Wash the watercress and keep a few leaves for garnish. Cut the potatoes into pieces and cook in the chicken stock for 25 minutes. Put into the blender with the watercress, cover and blend until smooth. Add the milk and the cornflour mixed with a little milk or water, and blend for 10 seconds. Reheat the soup, seasoning to taste, and garnish with reserved watercress leaves.

Chilled Apple Soup

1$\frac{1}{2}$*lb/600g cooking apples*
$\frac{1}{4}$ *pint/125ml white wine*
$\frac{1}{4}$ *pint/125ml single cream*
Sugar

The best apples to use are those which collapse into a fluffy purée when cooked, such as Bramley Seedlings. Peel and core the apples and cut them into slices. Put into a saucepan with just enough water to cover, and simmer until soft. Cool and put into the blender with the wine and cream. Blend until smooth and sweeten very lightly as the soup should be a little sharp to taste. For a garnish, a little finely grated lemon rind, or a sprinkle of cinnamon, adds flavour and colour.

Chilled Cherry Soup

¼ lemon
1lb/400g sweet black cherries
¾ pint/375ml water
2oz/50g honey
2fl.oz/50ml sherry
¼ teaspoon ground cinnamon

Remove pips from the lemon. Cut the lemon in pieces, including the skin, and blend with a little of the water until finely chopped. Remove the stones from the cherries, and put into a saucepan with the lemon, water, honey, sherry and cinnamon. Bring to the boil and simmer for 5 minutes. Cool and blend until the cherries are chopped into small pieces. Chill before serving, and if liked garnish with a little commercial sour cream.

Chilled Raspberry Soup

1lb/400g raspberries
4oz/100g sugar
2 teaspoons/10ml lemon juice
2oz/50g butter
1oz/25g plain flour
¼ teaspoon salt
Pinch of ground cinnamon
1 pint/500ml milk

Reserve a few raspberries for garnish. Put into the blender with the sugar and lemon juice and blend until completely crushed. Sieve to remove pips, and chill. Melt the butter, stir in the flour, salt and cinnamon, and gradually stir in the milk. Cook gently, stirring well, until the mixture begins to thicken. Cool and put into the blender with the raspberry purée. Blend until smooth, chill, and serve garnished with remaining raspberries.

Chilled Avocado Soup

2 medium avocadoes
¼ pint/125ml natural yogurt
2 garlic cloves
1 small onion
¾ pint/375ml milk

Use soft ripe avocadoes for this recipe, and make the soup about 1 hour before serving, so that there is time to chill it without taking away the delicate flavour. Cut the avocadoes in half and scoop out the flesh into the blender. Add the yogurt, peeled garlic cloves and onion cut into pieces. Add the milk and blend until completely smooth.

Chilled Beetroot Soup

1lb/400g cooked beetroot
1½ pints/750ml water
2 small lemons
3 standard eggs
1 teaspoon salt
1 tablespoon/15ml liquid
  honey

Peel the beetroot and cut into pieces. Put into the blender with water and blend until finely chopped. Put into a saucepan and bring to the boil. Meanwhile, peel the lemons and remove the pips. Cut the flesh into pieces and blend until smooth. Add to the beetroot, and simmer for 15 minutes. Take off the heat and cool for 10 minutes. In a bowl, mix the eggs, salt and honey, and gradually pour in the beetroot mixture. Stir well and serve cold. If liked, the soup can be returned to the blender when the eggs have been added, and blended until completely smooth.

Chilled Cucumber Soup

2 *large cucumbers*
1 *pint/500ml natural yogurt*
1 *teaspoon salt*
Pinch of nutmeg
2 *teaspoons fresh dill*

Trim the ends from the cucumbers, but do not peel them. Cut a few very thin slices to use as garnish. Cut the cucumbers into pieces and blend with the yogurt, salt, nutmeg and half the dill. Blend until smooth, and chill. Serve garnished with chopped dill and cucumber slices.

Chilled Tomato and Orange Soup

1 *pint/500ml tomato juice*
½ *pint/250ml orange juice*
Pinch of salt
1 *teaspoon sugar*
Mint leaves

Put the tomato and orange juices into the blender with the salt and sugar. Blend until completely mixed, and chill. Garnish with a few fresh mint leaves.

Gazpacho

1 *garlic clove*
1 *small onion*
1 *cucumber*
1 *pint/500ml tomato juice*
2 *tablespoons/30ml lemon juice*
3 *tablespoons/45ml olive oil*
¼ *pint/125ml iced water*
1 *teaspoon salt*
¼ *teaspoon Cayenne pepper*
1 *green pepper*
2 *tomatoes*

Cut up the garlic clove, onion and cucumber, reserving about one-third of the cucumber. Put all ingredients except green pepper, tomatoes and reserved cucumber into the blender and cover. Blend for 10 seconds. Pour into individual bowls and chill in the refrigerator. Put green pepper and cucumber into the blender, cover and blend for 5 seconds. Dip tomatoes in boiling water. Skin tomatoes, remove seeds, and chop flesh roughly by hand. Just before serving, add the pepper, cucumber and tomatoes to the bowls of soup, together with some toasted bread cubes.

Chestnut Soup

1 *medium onion*
1 *carrot*
2 *leeks*
3 *celery sticks*
2oz/50g *butter*
2 *pints/1 litre milk*
Salt and pepper
36 *chestnuts*

Cut the onion, carrot, leeks and celery sticks in pieces and chop finely in the blender in small quantities. Melt the butter and cook the vegetables gently until soft and golden. Add the milk and seasoning and simmer for 1 hour. Meanwhile shell and peel the chestnuts. Take half the liquid and simmer the chestnuts for 1½ hours. Keep 6 nuts aside to use for garnish, and put the remaining chestnuts, cooking liquid and vegetables into the blender. Blend until smooth and then simmer together for 10 minutes, adjusting seasoning to taste. Chop the reserved chestnuts roughly in the blender, and use to garnish the bowls of soup.

5 Pâtés

Pâtés made from meat, poultry, game or fish may be used as first courses, or can be a complete light meal served with salad or toast. They also make excellent sandwich fillings. If a grinder is available, raw meat can be chopped before cooking, but a blender is not suitable for processing raw meat. The mincer attachment may be used instead, but if this is also not available, the meat may be cooked lightly in a little butter and then blended with any liquids in the recipe, scraping down the mixture frequently to prevent the blender overworking.

It is worth making a large quantity of pâtés, as the process involves a fair amount of work and there is little point in making only a little for immediate use. Pâté freezes well, or can be stored in a refrigerator under a 'seal' of melted clarified butter or lard. Pâté may be cooked in a large earthenware terrine, but an ordinary casserole, cake tin or bread tin can be used, or a deep foil case, or individual pots. For freezer storage the pâté may be left in a foil case, or else turned out and wrapped in foil or polythene. The topping of fat should be omitted for freezer storage. Adjust the seasoning of pâté carefully, particularly if bacon is included since this can be very salty. Use sea salt and freshly ground black pepper, fresh herbs and spices. A little brandy or sherry will improve the flavour, and the meat or game can be left to marinade in this liquid before cooking.

A decorative finish improves the appearance of pâté. It is most simple to line the container with thin rashers of streaky bacon, flattened out with a wide-bladed knife. Under the bacon lining a pattern of bay leaves and juniper berries may be arranged. When the pâté is cold and turned out, the pattern will remain on the surface. If a pâté is to be served from its container, it can be finished with a layer of melted butter or lard and a sprig of parsley or a bay leaf. For a party, arrange thin lemon or orange slices on top of the pâté, or a row of mushroom slices, or a pattern of juniper berries and bay leaves and finish with a thin glaze of aspic jelly. Individual portions of fish pâté can be topped with a thin slice of cucumber or lemon and a little aspic jelly.

Bacon Pâté (1)

12oz/300g *unsmoked bacon rashers*
1lb/400g *lean pork*
1 *small onion*
6oz/150g *white bread*
2 *eggs*
2 *hard-boiled eggs*
Salt, pepper and nutmeg

Remove the rind from the bacon. Smooth out six of the rashers with a flat-bladed knife and line a loaf tin or casserole. Cut the rest in pieces and mix with the pork and onion cut in pieces. Chop finely in a grinder. Make the bread into crumbs in the blender. Mix with the meat and eggs. Chop the hard-boiled eggs coarsely in the blender and stir into the mixture. Season well and press into the lined container. Cover with greaseproof paper and foil and stand the container in a roasting tin of water. Bake at 350°F/180°C/Gas Mark 4 for 1¼ hours. Cool under weights. Serve in slices with salad or with toast. If preferred, the bacon, pork and onion may be minced instead of being processed in a grinder.

Bacon Pâté (2)

12oz/300g *bacon*
1 *medium onion*
2oz/50g *butter*
1 *tablespoon chopped parsley*
Pepper
2 *teaspoons/10ml made mustard*

This is a good pâté to make with bacon pieces, which contain a high proportion of fat. Fry or grill the bacon until cooked but not crisp, and put through a mincer. Chop the onion finely in the blender and then cook in the butter until soft and golden. Mix with the bacon and with the cooking juices. Add the parsley, plenty of pepper and the mustard. Mix very thoroughly and press into a serving dish. If a smooth mixture is preferred, blend all the ingredients after cooking. Chill before serving. For storage in the refrigerator, seal the top with a little clarified butter.

Chicken and Bacon Pâté

6oz/150g *cooked chicken*
4 *bacon rashers*
1 *small onion*
3oz/75g *full fat soft cheese*
½ *teaspoon mixed herbs*
Salt and pepper

Cut the chicken into pieces. Grill the bacon and cut into pieces. Peel the onion and cut it into pieces. Put all the ingredients into the blender and blend until smooth. If the mixture is a little stiff to blend, add a little sherry or milk.

Chicken and Ham Pâté

1oz/25g plain flour
½ pint/250ml milk
Salt and pepper
Pinch of nutmeg
1oz/25g butter
1 small onion
6oz/150g cooked chicken
6oz/150g cooked ham
Sprig of parsley
½ teaspoon/2.5ml made
  mustard
5 drops Worcestershire sauce

Put the flour, milk, salt and pepper and nutmeg into the blender and blend until smooth. Melt the butter and gradually pour in the milk mixture. Cook and stir gently until the sauce is smooth and thick. Cut the onion, chicken and ham into small pieces. Put the sauce into the blender and start to run the motor on low speed. Gradually add the onion, chicken and ham, parsley, mustard and Worcestershire sauce. When all the ingredients are incorporated, run the machine at high speed until the mixture is smooth. Put into a serving dish and chill before serving.

Chicken Liver Pâté

8oz/200g chicken livers
3oz/75g fat bacon
1 small onion
2 garlic cloves
1 egg
Salt and pepper

Cut the chicken livers, bacon and onion into pieces. Chop the livers finely in a grinder. Take out and chop the bacon and onion finely. Cook the bacon and onion in a little butter until just soft. Add the chicken livers and cook gently for 10 minutes. Put into the blender with garlic cloves, egg and seasoning, and blend until smooth. Put into a container, cover with greaseproof paper and a lid or foil, and then stand the container in a roasting tin of water. Cook at 350°F/180°C/Gas Mark 4 for 1 hour. Cool under a weight. Cover the surface with a little melted butter. Serve with crisp toast. If liked, the ingredients may be minced instead of being processed in a grinder before cooking.

Game Pâté

1½lb/600g uncooked game
4oz/100g fat bacon
3 tablespoons/45ml brandy
12oz/300g pork and veal
Salt, pepper and nutmeg
1 egg

Any mixture of game can be used for this pâté, but it is a good idea to have a mixture of light and dark meat. Use rabbit, hare, pheasant and pigeon, but if there is not much game available, use a little chicken as well. Cut the game into pieces and cut up the bacon. Chop together coarsely in a grinder. Put into a dish with the brandy for 1 hour. Chop the pork and veal finely together in the grinder and mix with seasoning and egg. Stir in the chopped game, bacon and brandy and put into a loaf tin or casserole. Cover with greaseproof paper and a lid or foil, and stand the dish in a roasting tin of water. Bake at 350°F/180°C/Gas Mark 4 for 1½ hours. Cool under weights. Serve in slices with salad or with toast. If a grinder is not available, chop half the game by hand, and mince the remainder with the pork and veal. Mix the minced meat and chopped meat before cooking.

Hazelnut Pâté

1lb/400g pig's liver
12oz/300g belly of pork
12oz/300g lard
Salt and pepper
1 garlic clove
3 tablespoons/45ml whisky
3 tablespoons/45ml water
4oz/100g unsalted shelled
  hazelnuts

Cut the liver and pork into pieces and chop finely in a grinder. Mix with slightly softened lard, salt and pepper, crushed garlic, whisky, 3 tablespoons water and hazelnuts. Leave to stand for 1 hour. Put into a container and cover with greaseproof paper and foil. Bake at 325°F/170°C/Gas Mark 3 for 2 hours. Leave until completely cold under a light weight. This pâté is best eaten after two or three days, and may be served in slices with salad or with toast.

Lamb Pâté

12oz/300g streaky bacon
  rashers
12oz/300g lamb's liver
1¾lb/750g shoulder lamb
1 large onion
1 garlic clove
1 tablespoon tomato purée
1 teaspoon sage
1 teaspoon rosemary
Salt and pepper
4oz/100g melted butter
¼ pint/125ml red wine

Remove the rind from the bacon rashers and stretch the rashers with a flat-bladed knife. Line a casserole or terrine with them. Mince the liver, lamb, onion and garlic together. Mix with the remaining ingredients and put into the bacon-lined dish. Fold the bacon over the top and cover with foil. Bake at 350°F/180°C/Gas Mark 4 for 1½ hours. Cool under weights for 24 hours. If liked, decorate with thin orange slices and a thin glaze of aspic jelly.

Lamb's Liver Pâté

1lb/400g lamb's liver
4oz/100g butter
1 medium onion
4 bacon rashers
¼ teaspoon thyme
1 bay leaf
2 tablespoons/30ml brandy
2 tablespoons/30ml dry sherry
2½fl.oz/65ml double cream
2 tablespoons chopped parsley
Salt and pepper

Cut the liver into thin slices and cook gently in a little of the butter until brown. Take out the liver. Chop the onion and bacon in the blender and cook in the butter with the thyme and bay leaf until the onion is transparent. Return the liver to the pan and cook for 5 minutes. Take off the heat and discard the bay leaf. Put the contents of the pan into the blender with the remaining ingredients and blend until smooth. Press into a dish and chill for 24 hours before serving. If liked, seal with a little melted clarified butter.

Quick Liver Pâté

3oz/75g full fat soft cheese
4oz/100g liver sausage
1oz/25g tomato chutney
Salt and pepper
1 tablespoon/15ml sherry

Cut the cheese and liver sausage into pieces. Put all the ingredients into the blender, and blend until smooth and well mixed. Chill before serving. There are various types of liver sausage available, and it is best to choose Continental-style sausage, which is very soft and easily blended.

Rich Liver Pâté

12oz/300g pig's liver
5 anchovies
1 small onion
2oz/50g breadcrumbs
$\frac{3}{4}$ pint/375ml milk
8oz/200g lard
2oz/50g butter
2oz/50g plain flour
1 large egg
$\frac{1}{2}$oz/15g salt
$\frac{1}{2}$oz/15g pepper
1 teaspoon mixed spice
1 teaspoon ground cloves
$\frac{1}{2}$ teaspoon sugar

Cut the liver into pieces. Drain the anchovies, and cut the onion into pieces. Mince the liver, anchovies and onion, using the fine screen of the mixer attachment. Soak the crumbs in a little of the milk. Put the liver mixture through the mincer again with the soaked crumbs and the lard. Melt the butter, work in the flour, and cook gently for 3 minutes, stirring well. Add the rest of the milk and cook gently, stirring all the time to make a thick sauce. Cool and then put into the blender with the meat mixture, egg and seasonings. Blend until smooth. Put into an ovenware dish, cover and stand the dish in a roasting tin containing 1in/2.5cm water. Cook at 350°F/180°C/Gas Mark 4 for 2 hours. Remove the lid, and cool under a weight for 24 hours.

Pigeon Pâté

3 young pigeons
8fl.oz/200ml red wine
4fl.oz/100ml vinegar
1 bay leaf
1 teaspoon thyme
Salt, pepper and nutmeg
2 large onions
8oz/200g pork sausagemeat
1 thick slice bread
A little milk

Remove legs from the pigeons and cut their bodies in half. Put into a deep dish and cover with the red wine, vinegar, herbs and seasonings. Chop the onions finely in the blender and add to the mixture. Cover and leave in the refrigerator for 3 days. Take the flesh from the pigeons and mince twice to a fine consistency. Mix with the sausagemeat. Take the crusts off the bread and soak the bread in just enough milk to moisten. Add to the meat mixture, together with a little of the marinade and 2 tablespoonsful of the onion. Press into an ovenware dish and cover with foil or a lid. Stand the dish in a tin of water and cook at 350°F/180°C/Gas Mark 4 for 1½ hours. Cool under weights and leave for 24 hours before serving.

Pork and Liver Pâté

12oz/300g *pig's liver*
2lb/1kg *belly of pork*
1 *large onion*
1 *large sprig parsley*
1 *large egg*
½ oz/15g *flour*
Salt, pepper and nutmeg
4oz/100g *streaky bacon*
  rashers

Cut the liver and pork into pieces and put into a grinder in small quantities together with the peeled onion and parsley. Chop finely. Mix with the egg, flour and seasonings. Cut the rinds from the bacon and flatten the rashers with a broad-bladed knife. Line a casserole or loaf tin with bacon rashers and put in the meat mixture. Cover with greaseproof paper and a lid or foil. Put the container into a roasting tin with 1in/2.5cm water and cook at 350°F/180°C/Gas Mark 4 for 1¾ hours. Cool under weights.

Terrine of Pork

12oz/300g *lean pork*
4oz/100g *fat pork*
4oz/100g *pig's liver*
1 *small onion*
1 *garlic clove*
2oz/50g *day-old bread*
1 *large egg*
4 *sage leaves*
Sprig of rosemary
Salt, pepper and nutmeg
1 *tablespoon/15ml brandy or*
  dry sherry

Mince the lean and fat pork, liver, onion and garlic twice, using the fine screen of the mixer attachment. Break the bread into small pieces and make breadcrumbs in the blender. Put all the ingredients into the blender and blend slowly until smooth. Press firmly into an ovenware dish. Cover with a piece of greaseproof paper and a lid, and put the dish into a roasting tin containing about 1in/2.5cm water. Cook at 325°F/170°C/Gas Mark 3 for 2½ hours. Take off the lid and paper, and cover again with some buttered paper. Put on a weight and leave for 24 hours.

Potted Rabbit

1 *rabbit*
10oz/250g *butter*
1 *teaspoon sugar*
1 *medium onion*
12 *cloves*
12 *allspice*
6 *peppercorns*
Grating of nutmeg
2 *teaspoons/10ml*
  Worcestershire sauce

Cut the rabbit into joints and put into a casserole with a tight-fitting lid. Put in 2oz/50g butter, sugar, onion stuck with the cloves, allspice, peppercorns and nutmeg. Cover and cook at 300°F/150°C/Gas Mark 2 for 3 hours. Cool and remove the rabbit meat from the bones. Put through the mincer twice with the juices from the casserole. Beat in the remaining butter and sauce and put into individual pots. Cool and cover with melted clarified butter.

Rillettes

6lb/3kg pork belly
2 cloves
4oz/100g sea salt
1 teaspoon pepper
Parsley, thyme and bay leaf
8fl.oz/200ml water

Cut the pork into pieces and then chop coarsely in a grinder. Put into a heavy saucepan with the cloves, salt and pepper, herbs and water. Cook over the lowest possible heat for 5 hours, stirring occasionally to prevent the meat sticking to the bottom. With a wooden spoon, squash the meat until it forms a paste in which pieces of meat cannot be found. When the mixture has reached this stage, continue cooking for 15 minutes. Cool slightly, then put into jars or dishes and smooth the surfaces. Cover with a layer of melted lard to store. To serve, rillettes should be at room temperature, and the mixture is delicious on hot toast.

Cod's Roe Pâté

12oz/300g smoked cod's roe
Juice of $\frac{1}{2}$ lemon
1 tablespoon/15ml olive oil
1 garlic clove
Black pepper
$\frac{1}{4}$ pint/125ml double cream

Scrape the roe from the skin. Put into the blender with lemon juice, oil, chopped garlic and pepper. Cover and blend for 10 seconds. Scrape down mixture and pour in cream. Cover and blend for 5 seconds. Put into an oiled dish and chill before serving.

Kipper Pâté

8oz/200g kipper fillets
1oz/25g butter
Juice of $\frac{1}{2}$ lemon
1 garlic clove
1 tablespoon/15ml brandy
4 drops Tabasco sauce
2 tablespoons/30ml single
  cream

Cook the kippers by grilling or poaching them. Remove skin and larger bones. Break the flesh into the blender with melted butter, lemon juice, garlic clove, brandy and Tabasco sauce. Blend until smooth. Add the cream and blend for 2 seconds. Put into a serving dish and chill before serving.

Sardine Pâté

$3\frac{1}{2}$oz/90g can sardines
5oz/125g full fat soft cheese
Salt and pepper
1 tablespoon/15ml lemon
  juice
2 hard-boiled eggs

Put the sardines and their oil into the blender with the cream cheese cut in pieces. Add the salt and pepper and lemon juice and blend until just mixed. Cut the eggs in pieces and add to the blender, and blend until the eggs are finely chopped. Put into a serving dish and chill before serving.

Seafood Pâté

1lb/400g fresh shrimps or
  prawns
1lb/400g haddock
1 teaspoon/5ml anchovy
  essence
Pinch of mace
Pinch of Cayenne pepper
12oz/300g unsalted butter

Shell the shrimps or prawns. Put the shells in a saucepan with a little water for 20 seconds. Strain the liquid and use this for cooking the haddock for 10 minutes. Put the shrimps or prawns into the blender, and chop, but do not purée. Remove from the blender. Put the haddock into the blender with the essence and spices. Reserve 2oz/50g butter, and soften the remainder without melting. Put the softened butter into the blender, and blend fish mixture until smooth. Remove from blender and stir in the chopped shrimps. Put into a serving dish. Cool and then cover with the remaining melted butter.

Smoked Fish Pâté

2 smoked trout or mackerel
¼ pint/125ml sour cream
4oz/100g cottage cheese
Juice of ½ lemon
Salt and pepper

Skin the fish and remove the flesh. Put into the grinder and chop finely. Put the fish into the blender with the other ingredients and blend until smooth. Put into small individual dishes and chill. Serve with thin slices of toast made from brown bread, and slices of lemon.

Smoked Haddock Pâté

8oz/200g smoked haddock
  fillet
1oz/25g plain flour
8fl.oz/200ml milk
Salt and pepper
3oz/75g butter
½ pint/250ml aspic
2 tablespoons/30ml single
  cream
1 tablespoon/15ml sherry

Poach the haddock in a little water for 10 minutes. Drain well, remove skin, and break the flesh into pieces. Put the flour, milk and seasoning into the blender and blend until smooth. Melt 1oz/25g butter in a saucepan, and gently stir in the milk mixture. Cook and stir gently until the sauce is smooth and thick. Cool to lukewarm. Make up the aspic from a packet of crystals, and cool. Soften the remaining butter, but do not melt. Put the fish into the blender with the white sauce, half the liquid aspic, cream, sherry and softened butter, and blend until smooth. Put into a serving dish and chill for 30 minutes. Pour over the remaining aspic liquid and chill until set. If liked, the top of the pâté may be decorated with thin slices of cucumber and/or a few shrimps or prawns before the final coating of aspic is poured on.

Smoked Salmon Pâté

1lb/400g smoked salmon
  trimmings
2oz/50g unsalted butter
1 tablespoon/15ml dry sherry
1 tablespoon/15ml lemon
  juice
Pinch of pepper
$\frac{1}{4}$ pint/125ml double cream

Cut the salmon in small pieces. Put into blender with butter, sherry, lemon juice and pepper. Cover and blend for 10 seconds. Scrape down mixture and pour in cream. Cover and blend for 5 seconds. Put into an oiled dish and chill before serving.

6 Main Courses and Salads

The range of main courses which can be prepared with a mixer and blender is extremely wide. If a mincer and shredder are also available, the range will be extended still further. Apart from the sauces that can be produced to accompany main dishes (see Chapter Seven), there are stuffings for meat, fish and vegetables, which can be made in the blender. Breadcrumbs and grated cheese can be prepared for toppings, batters whipped up, and mixer-made pastry used.

Meat
Extend helpings with sauces, stuffings, pastry or batters, or use these additions to make the best of leftovers. Use a mincer or blender to produce meat loaves, mousses, croquettes from a few scraps of cooked meat or poultry.

Fish
Good fish dishes can be baked in the oven with a topping of crumbs, cheese, onions or tomatoes to give added flavour and texture. Sauces may be made in the blender to serve with plainly grilled or fried fish, and cooked fish can be smoothed in the blender to use in mousses, croquettes and soufflés.

Pastry dishes
Using mixer-made pastry, a wide variety of flans may be made using fresh or cooked ingredients chopped or puréed in the blender, perhaps accompanied with blender-made sauce, or egg and milk mixture. Cheese can be chopped for toppings. Small amounts of leftover meat, poultry or fish can be blended with sauce and used as fillings for turnovers or pasties.

Cheese

A little cheese gives flavour and colour to many main courses. Complete cheese dishes and cheese sauces can be quickly made with the blender. Only process cheese in small quantities of about 2oz/50g, cut in small pieces. Hard dry cheese should be blended in a dry goblet at high speed. Soft cheese is best blended with a dry ingredient such as flour or bread, which will absorb oil and prevent the cheese packing together during blending.

Eggs

A blender is useful for egg dishes as the speed may be regulated to give a lightly-beaten or a well-beaten mixture. Fillings may be chopped with the eggs for omelettes, or separate fillings and sauces can be made. Batters of all thicknesses for pancakes or batter puddings can be speedily prepared with the blender, or whipped up quickly with the mixer. Soufflés present no hazards when the sauce is prepared in the blender, complete with chopped or puréed flavourings, and the egg whites can be whisked to stiff peaks with the mixer.

Apricot Pork with Apple Sauce

4oz/100g white bread
Sprig of parsley
1 × 15oz/375g can apricot
  halves
½ teaspoon fresh mixed herbs
1 egg
Salt and pepper
4lb/2kg boned pork joint
12oz/300g cooking apples
1oz/25g demerara sugar

Make breadcrumbs in the blender, adding the parsley with the last batch of bread. Put into a mixing bowl. Drain the apricots and blend half of them until they are roughly chopped. Mix with bread, herbs, egg and seasonings and stir well. Stuff the meat and put it into a roasting tin. Pour over the apricot syrup and cook at 375°F/190°C/Gas Mark 5 for 2½ hours, basting with syrup once or twice. Peel and core the apples and chop them roughly in the blender. Put into a saucepan with 6 tablespoons/90ml water and demerara sugar and cook until soft. Put into the blender and add the remaining apricots. Blend until smooth and reheat just before serving with the pork.

Shepherd's Pie

1lb/400g cooked beef or lamb
1 medium onion
¼ pint/125ml stock
Salt and pepper
1lb/400g mashed potato

Cut the meat into pieces and chop finely in the blender with the onion, stock and seasoning and put into an ovenware dish. Cover with the mashed potato and brush with a little melted butter, lard or dripping. Bake at 400°F/200°C/Gas Mark 6 for 45 minutes. Serve with additional gravy if liked. For extra flavouring, a little tomato purée or a pinch of mixed herbs may be added.

Meat Balls

12oz/300g *frying steak*
4oz/100g *lean pork*
2oz/50g *dry white bread*
½ *pint/250ml creamy milk*
1 *small onion*
1oz/25g *butter*
1 *teaspoon salt*
¼ *teaspoon pepper*
Butter for frying

Cut the steak and pork in pieces and chop finely in a grinder. Make breadcrumbs in the blender and soak in the milk. Peel the onion and cut in pieces, then chop finely in the blender. Cook the onion in butter until golden and mix together with the meat, breadcrumbs and seasonings until well blended. Shape into 1in/2.5cm balls, using two tablespoons dipped in cold water. Fry the balls in butter until evenly browned, shaking pan to keep balls round. Cook a few at a time, draining each batch. Serve in gravy or tomato sauce. Meat balls in tomato sauce are excellent with spaghetti.

Beef Olives

1lb/500g *braising steak*
1 *large onion*
1oz/25g *dripping*
3oz/75g *fresh white bread*
Grated rind and juice of ½
  lemon
1 *egg*
Salt and pepper
½ *teaspoon sage*
½ *pint/250ml stock*
½oz/15g *cornflour*

Cut the steak into four slices and flatten them with a rolling pin. Peel the onion, cut it in pieces, and chop finely in the blender. Cook the onion lightly in the dripping. Make breadcrumbs in the blender. Add grated lemon rind and juice, egg, salt, pepper and sage to the blender, and work until well mixed. Divide the mixture between the pieces of steak, and roll up each steak around the stuffing, tying with cotton. Take the onion out of the fat and brown the meat rolls in the remaining fat. Return the onion to the pan, add stock, cover and simmer for 1½ hours. Put the meat rolls on a serving dish. Blend cornflour with a little water, stir into the stock and cook for 3 minutes, stirring well. Pour over the beef olives. If preferred, serve the beef olives in tomato sauce.

Sweet and Sour Pork

1½lb/600g *lean pork*
Juice of ½ *lemon*
1 *egg*
4oz/100g *plain flour*
¼ *pint/125ml milk*
Salt and pepper
Deep fat for frying
Sweet and Sour Sauce (see
  page 71)

Cut the pork into 1in/2.5cm cubes and leave in a bowl with the lemon juice for 30 minutes. Put the egg, flour, milk and seasoning into the blender and blend until creamy and smooth. Drain the pork pieces, dip in the batter and fry until golden brown and crisp. Drain on kitchen paper and serve with Sweet and Sour Sauce.

Corned Beef Pie

12oz/300g *shortcrust pastry*
2oz/50g *white bread*
2oz/50g *Cheddar cheese*
2 tablespoons *parsley*
1 *small onion*
6oz/150g *corned beef*
½ teaspoon *Worcestershire sauce*
3 tablespoons/45ml *milk*
Salt and pepper

Roll out the pastry and use half to line an 8in/20cm heatproof plate. Break up the bread and make into breadcrumbs in the blender adding the cheese and parsley during the final blending. Put into a bowl. Cut the onion and corned beef in pieces and put into the blender with the Worcestershire sauce, milk and seasoning. Blend until the onion is finely chopped. Mix with the breadcrumbs and put into the pastry case. Moisten the edges of the pastry and cover with the other half, sealing the edges well. Brush with a little milk and bake at 400°F/200°C/Gas Mark 6 for 45 minutes. Serve hot or cold.

Baked Gammon in Apple Sauce

1lb/400g *gammon steak*
1oz/25g *butter*
3 *medium onions*
¼ pint/125ml *dry cider*
2 *medium cooking apples*
2oz/50g *soft brown sugar*
1 teaspoon *mustard powder*
Pepper
3 *cloves*

Have the gammon cut about 2in/5cm thick and put into an ovenware dish well-greased with the butter. Cut the onions in pieces and put into the blender with the cider, peeled and cored apples, sugar, mustard and pepper. Blend until the onions and apples are finely chopped. Pour over the gammon and add the cloves. Cover with foil and bake at 350°F/180°C/Gas Mark 4 for 1 hour. Uncover the gammon, remove cloves and continue baking for 15 minutes.

Pennywise Lamb Roast

1 *breast of lamb*
2 teaspoons *made mustard*
4oz/100g *soft white bread*
1 tablespoon *fresh mint or parsley*
½ teaspoon *mixed herbs*
1 *small onion*
Salt and pepper
1 *egg*

Remove the bones from the lamb, or get the butcher to do this. Score any skin with a sharp knife, cutting just through the skin and no deeper. Spread the mustard over the meat. Break the bread in small pieces and make into crumbs with the blender. Put into a bowl. Put the mint or parsley, herbs and roughly chopped onion into the blender with the seasoning and egg, and blend until the onion is finely chopped. Pour on to the breadcrumbs and mix well. Spread this stuffing on the meat and roll it up, tying securely. Brown on all sides in a little hot fat. Bake at 400°F/200°C/Gas Mark 6 for 15 minutes, then at 350°F/180°C/Gas Mark 4 for 1¼ hours. Serve with a rich brown gravy and oven-baked jacket potatoes. Boiled butter beans or haricot beans dressed with butter and chopped parsley are also good with lamb.

Braised Lamb Shoulder

3lb/1.5kg boned lamb
  shoulder
8oz/200g onions
1 garlic clove
4oz/100g lean bacon
2oz/50g butter
8oz/200g carrots
4oz/100g turnips
2 celery sticks
¼ pint/125ml red wine
¼ pint/125ml water
1 teaspoon rosemary
Salt and pepper

Roll up the lamb shoulder and tie firmly. Chop the onions, garlic and bacon in the blender coarsely and cook in the butter until the onion is soft and golden. Put the carrots, turnips and celery into the blender with wine, water and rosemary. Blend until the ingredients are coarsely chopped. Season and mix with the onion mixture. Bring to the boil and pour into a casserole. Put the lamb shoulder on top, cover and simmer gently for 2–2½ hours until the lamb is tender. The casserole may be cooked at 350°F/180°C/Gas Mark 4 for 2 hours instead. Just before serving, strain off the cooking liquid and boil until reduced by half. Pour over the meat and vegetables.

Braised Chops

4 large lamb or pork chops
1oz/25g plain flour
Salt and pepper
1oz/25g lard
4 medium potatoes
1 large onion
2 celery sticks
8oz/200g tomatoes
2 teaspoons sugar
1 teaspoon Worcestershire
  sauce

Toss the chops in flour seasoned with salt and pepper. Fry on both sides in the lard until the chops are crisp and golden. Grease an ovenware dish. Peel the potatoes and cut in thin slices. Arrange potato slices in the dish. Put the chopped onion and celery in the blender. Peel the tomatoes and remove the pips. Put the flesh into the blender with the sugar and sauce, and blend until the onion and celery are finely chopped. Season and pour over the potatoes. Put the chops on top. Cover with a lid or foil and bake at 350°F/180°C/Gas Mark 4 for 1¼ hours.

Lamburgers

1 large onion
1oz/25g butter
1lb/400g shoulder lamb
1 small green pepper
1 celery stick
1 tablespoon tomato purée
1 tablespoon tomato sauce
1 teaspoon mixed herbs
½ teaspoon Worcestershire
  sauce
Salt and pepper
2oz/50g fresh white
  breadcrumbs

Cut the onion in pieces and blend until finely chopped. Cook gently in the butter until soft and golden but not brown. Mince the lamb, and chop the green pepper and celery finely in the blender. Mix all the ingredients together. Turn on to a floured board and divide into eight pieces. Shape into thick patties. Fry in oil on both sides until golden brown, which will take about 10–15 minutes. Serve with vegetables or salad. If liked, put each hot lamburger into a warm split soft roll and garnish with tomatoes and watercress.

Lamb in Cider

2lb/1kg lamb shoulder
  (without bone)
1oz/25g plain flour
2oz/50g butter
2 small onions
1 garlic clove
2 tablespoons parsley
¼ pint/125ml stock
¼ pint/125ml dry cider
1 tablespoon/15ml
  Worcestershire sauce
Salt and pepper

Cut the meat into cubes and coat lightly with the flour. Fry in the butter until brown on all sides. Peel the onions and garlic clove, and chop the onions, garlic and parsley in the blender with the stock, cider, sauce and seasoning, until the onions are finely chopped. Simmer for 5 minutes, and pour over the meat in a casserole. Cover and cook at 325°F/170°C/Gas Mark 3 for 1½ hours.

Liver Casserole

1lb/500g lamb's or pig's liver
1oz/25g plain flour
2oz/50g butter
2 medium onions
Salt and pepper
8oz/200g fresh white bread
2 tablespoons parsley
½ pint/250ml water

Cut the liver in slices, toss in flour and brown lightly in the butter. Cut the onions in pieces and chop them in the blender. Put a layer of liver in an ovenware dish, top with onions and sprinkle with salt and pepper. Continue in layers, finishing with a layer of onions. Make breadcrumbs in the blender, adding the parsley with the last batch of bread. Cover the liver and onions with the crumb and parsley mixture and pour on the water. Cover and cook at 350°F/180°C/Gas Mark 4 for 45 minutes. Remove the lid and continue cooking for 15 minutes.

Savoury Chicken

4 chicken pieces
¾ pint/375ml stock
1 medium onion
2 rashers streaky bacon
4 tomatoes
Peel of ¼ lemon
Blade of mace
Salt and pepper
4oz/100g Patna rice

Brown the chicken pieces in a little oil and drain well. Put the stock, onion and bacon in the blender. Peel the tomatoes and remove the pips, and add to the blender. Blend until the onion and bacon are finely chopped. Put into a saucepan with the lemon peel, mace and seasoning, and bring to the boil. Add the chicken pieces, cover and simmer for 35 minutes. Add the rice and cook for 25 minutes. Remove the lemon peel and mace, and serve hot.

Chicken in Curry Sauce

4 *chicken pieces*
2 *medium onions*
1oz/25g *butter*
1oz/25g *curry powder*
1 *pint/500ml chicken stock*
  (from cooking chicken
  pieces)
½oz/15g *cornflour*
1 *tablespoon/15ml vinegar*
½oz/15g *soft brown sugar*
1 *tablespoon/15ml sweet*
  chutney
1oz/25g *sultanas*

Simmer the chicken pieces in water until tender. Drain off the stock, reserving it in a bowl, and keep the chicken warm. Peel the onions and chop coarsely in the blender. Melt the butter and cook the onions until soft but not brown. Add the curry powder and cook for 1 minute. Put the reserved chicken stock and cornflour in the blender with the vinegar, sugar and chutney. Blend until smooth, add to the onions and simmer for 5 minutes. Put in the chicken pieces and sultanas and simmer for 15 minutes. Serve on a bed of rice.

Cod in Tomato Sauce

4 *cod steaks*
1 *large onion*
4oz/100g *streaky bacon*
1 *green pepper*
1 *tablespoon/15ml oil*
1 × 15oz/375g *can tomatoes*
½ *teaspoon mixed herbs*
Salt and pepper

Grill or fry the cod steaks and place in an ovenware dish. Peel the onion and cut in pieces, and cut up the bacon and pepper. Put into the blender and chop coarsely. Fry in the oil until soft and golden. Add the tomatoes with their juice, herbs and seasoning and simmer for 10 minutes. Pour over the cod steaks and bake at 325°F/170°C/Gas Mark 3 for 20 minutes.

Stuffed Green Peppers

4 *green peppers*
2 *medium slices bread*
8oz/200g *cooked ham or*
  bacon
Pinch of salt
Pinch of mustard powder
1 *small onion*
2 *eggs*
1 *tablespoon parsley*

Cut slices from the stem end of each pepper and remove the seeds and membranes. Cook the peppers in salted water for 5 minutes, drain well and put into an ovenware dish. Put small pieces of bread into the blender and make breadcrumbs. Remove to a bowl. Cut up the ham or bacon and chop very finely in the blender with the salt, mustard, onion, eggs and parsley. Mix with the breadcrumbs and fill the green peppers. Cover the dish and bake at 350°F/180°C/Gas Mark 4 for 40 minutes. Serve hot with tomato sauce.

Sicilian Chicken

4 *chicken joints*
Salt and pepper
4 *tablespoons/60ml olive oil*
2 *teaspoons marjoram*
3 *tablespoons/45ml lemon*
 juice
1 *garlic clove*
1 *teaspoon parsley*

Wipe the chicken joints and sprinkle them with salt and pepper. Put the oil, marjoram, lemon juice, chopped garlic and parsley into the blender and blend until the herbs are finely chopped. Brush this mixture generously on the chicken pieces on both sides. Put into a grill pan about 6in/15cm from the heat and grill for about 20 minutes on each side until brown and tender, turning once only, and sometimes brushing with the mixture. Heat any remaining sauce and pour over the hot chicken to serve. This is good with a green salad or it can be served with fried potatoes and peas or French beans.

Stuffed Tomatoes

4 *large tomatoes*
2oz/50g *white bread*
1 *small onion*
1 *tablespoon parsley*
2oz/50g *butter*
Salt and pepper

Cut the tops of the tomatoes to form 'lids' and keep on one side. Scoop out the pulp from the tomatoes and put into a bowl, removing as many pips as possible. Break the bread into small pieces and make into breadcrumbs in the blender, adding the chopped onion and parsley during the final blending until the onion is finely chopped. Put into the bowl with the tomato pulp and add melted butter and seasoning. Leave to stand for 10 minutes, then put into the tomato cases. Put back the 'lids'. Arrange in a lightly greased ovenware dish and bake at 400°F/200°C/Gas Mark 6 for 15 minutes. Serve hot.

Ham Tomatoes
Add 2oz/50g finely chopped cooked ham and ½ teaspoon made mustard.

Lamb Tomatoes
Add 2oz/50g finely chopped lean lamb and ½ teaspoon mixed herbs.

Cheese Tomatoes
Add 2oz/50g cheese to final blending.

Prawn Tomatoes
Substitute 2oz/50g peeled prawns for the onion.

Stuffed Cod Cutlets

4oz/100g *white bread*
1 *tablespoon parsley*
½ *teaspoon mixed herbs*
Salt and pepper
½ *lemon*
1 *egg*
2oz/50g *butter*
4 *cod cutlets*
1 *tomato*
½ *pint/500ml parsley sauce*

Break up the bread and make into crumbs in the blender, adding the parsley and herbs during the blending. Put into a bowl with the salt and pepper and add the grated rind and juice of the lemon, egg and half the melted butter. Remove the centre bone from each cutlet with a sharp knife. Use a little of the remaining butter to grease an ovenware dish and put in the cod cutlets. Fill the centre of each one with the prepared stuffing. Skin the tomato, cut it in slices and put slices on each cod cutlet. Pour a little melted butter on each one. Bake at 350°F/180°C/Gas Mark 4 for 30 minutes. Serve with hot parsley sauce (see page 68).

Honeyed Almond Roast Chicken

1oz/25g *dried apricots*
1oz/25g *blanched almonds*
1 *small onion*
1oz/25g *butter*
2oz/50g *white bread*
½ *teaspoon thyme*
1 *tablespoon/15ml clear
  honey*
1 *egg*
3–4lb/1.5–2kg *chicken*
1 *tablespoon/15ml oil*
Pinch of salt
Sprig of rosemary

Soak the apricots in water for 3 hours and drain. Put the apricots and almonds in the blender and blend on low speed until the almonds are finely chopped. Remove from blender and put into a bowl. Chop the onion in the blender and cook until soft and golden in the butter. Add to the bowl with the apricots. Break the bread into small pieces and put into the blender with the thyme. Blend to make breadcrumbs. Put into the bowl and add the honey. Mix together and add about half the egg to make a light crumbly stuffing. Put the stuffing in the neck end of the bird under the skin flap. Brush the chicken with the oil, sprinkle with salt and put the sprig of rosemary on top. Cover in foil and bake at 400°F/200°C/Gas Mark 6 allowing 20 minutes per lb/.5kg and 20 minutes extra. Take off the foil 15 minutes before the end of cooking time to allow the bird to brown.

Cheese and Onion Casserole

6 *slices white bread*
6oz/150g *Cheddar cheese*
3 *eggs*
Salt and pepper
1 *small onion*
¾ *pint/375ml milk*

Remove the crusts from the bread and cut the bread into triangles. Put half the triangles into a greased ovenware dish. Grate the cheese and sprinkle two-thirds of it over the bread. Cover with the remaining bread triangles. Put the eggs, seasoning, chopped onion and lukewarm milk into the blender, and blend until the onion is finely chopped. Pour over the bread and leave to stand for 30 minutes. Sprinkle on the remaining cheese, bake at 350°F/180°C/Gas Mark 4 for 1 hour until well browned, and serve very hot.

Stuffed Liver

12oz/300g lamb's or pig's
    liver
2oz/50g fresh white bread
1 small onion
1 sprig parsley
1 small egg
½ teaspoon/12.5ml
    Worcestershire sauce
6 rashers streaky bacon
½ pint/250ml stock

Cut the liver in thin slices and put into a greased ovenware dish. Put the bread into the blender and blend into crumbs. Put the breadcrumbs into a bowl. Peel the onion, cut it into pieces and put into the blender with the parsley, egg and Worcestershire sauce. Cover and blend until the parsley is chopped finely. Add this mixture to the breadcrumbs and mix well. Put this stuffing on top of the liver slices, and cover with bacon rashers. Pour on the stock. Bake at 350°F/180°C/Gas Mark 4 for 40 minutes.

Baked Stuffed Mackerel

4 mackerel
1 onion
1oz/25g butter
1 apple
3oz/75g fresh white bread
½ teaspoon mixed herbs
Grated rind and juice of ½
    lemon
Salt and pepper
Lemon slices and parsley for
    garnish

Open each fish and press out the backbone. Peel the onion and chop it finely in the blender. Cook in the butter until soft but not coloured. Peel the apple and chop it in the blender. Make breadcrumbs in the blender. Mix together the onion, apple, breadcrumbs, herbs, lemon rind and juice, salt and pepper. Divide the stuffing between the fish, and roll up from the wide end, securing with a cocktail stick. Put in an ovenware dish and brush each fish with a little oil. Cover with a piece of foil or a lid and bake at 350°F/180°C/Gas Mark 4 for 30 minutes. Remove foil or lid and continue cooking for 5 minutes. Serve garnished with lemon slices and sprigs of parsley, and with thin brown bread and butter.

Stuffed Whole Plaice

1 small onion
2oz/50g mushrooms
1oz/25g butter
2oz/50g fresh white bread
Salt and pepper
2 small whole plaice
Lemon slices and parsley for
    garnish

Cut the onion in pieces and chop the onion and mushrooms finely in the blender. Melt the butter and cook the onion and mushrooms until the onion is soft but not coloured. Make breadcrumbs in the blender. Mix the onion, mushrooms, breadcrumbs, salt and pepper. Skin the fish and make a cut down the centre of one side of each. Fill the cut with stuffing, and put in a greased ovenware dish. Bake at 400°F/200°C/Gas Mark 6 for 30 minutes. Serve garnished with lemon slices and parsley.

Chicken and Ham Loaf

6oz/150g cooked chicken
6oz/150g cooked ham
1 small onion
½ pint/250ml milk
Pinch of nutmeg
Salt and pepper
1oz/25g plain flour
1oz/25g softened butter
2 teaspoons parsley
½ teaspoon/12.5ml made
  mustard
½ teaspoon/12.5ml
  Worcestershire sauce

Cut the chicken and ham into pieces, chop finely in the blender and put into a bowl. Peel the onion and cut it into pieces. Chop the onion finely in the blender with the milk, nutmeg, salt and pepper, flour and butter. Blend until smooth, then cook gently until thick. Return to the blender with the chicken and ham, parsley, mustard and sauce, and blend until well mixed but not smooth. Put into a loaf tin or pudding basin and chill for 1 hour. Turn out to serve with salad.

Chicken Mousse

12fl.oz/300ml chicken stock
1oz/25g gelatine
Salt and pepper
1 thin slice onion
2 eggs
2oz/50g almonds
8oz/200g cooked chicken
8fl.oz/200ml double cream

Bring the stock to the boil, and put half into the blender with the gelatine, salt and pepper and onion. Blend until smooth. Add the eggs, almonds, and coarsely chopped chicken. Blend on high speed, gradually adding the cream until the mixture is smooth. Pour into a mould and chill until set.

Ham Loaf

1lb/400g cooked ham
½oz/15g gelatine
4fl.oz/100ml boiling water
1 tablespoon/15ml lemon
  juice
Pinch of pepper
2 sticks celery
1 small green pepper
1 thin slice onion
8fl.oz/200ml tomato juice

Cut the ham into small pieces and blend in small quantities until very finely chopped. Remove to a bowl. Put the gelatine and water into the blender and blend at high speed until well mixed, then add the lemon juice, pinch of pepper, celery, pepper and onion. Blend until the vegetables are finely chopped. Pour on to the ham with the tomato juice and mix well. Pour into a mould and chill before serving.

Opposite: Asparagus Soup (page 21).

Hot Savoury Loaf

1 *Vienna loaf*
1oz/25g *melted butter*
1 *small onion*
2 *lean bacon rashers*
2oz/50g *mushrooms*
1 *small green pepper*
6oz/150g *cooked chicken*
3oz/75g *full fat soft cheese*
2 *tablespoons/30ml milk*
Salt and pepper

Cut a 'lid' from the top of the loaf and scoop out most of the soft bread (use this for breadcrumbs for another dish). Replace the lid, wrap in foil and heat at 400°F/200°C/Gas Mark 6 for 15 minutes. Meanwhile melt the butter and cook the onion, bacon, mushrooms and pepper, which have been finely chopped in the blender. Put into the blender with the chicken cut in small pieces, cheese, milk and seasoning, and blend until the chicken is finely chopped. Heat gently and fill the loaf with the mixture. Serve hot.

Pork Loaf

4oz/100g *white bread*
¼ *pint/125ml milk*
2 *eggs*
1 *teaspoon Worcestershire
   sauce*
1 *medium onion*
1 *garlic clove*
½ *teaspoon mixed herbs*
Salt and pepper
12oz/300g *cooked pork*

Break the bread into pieces and make into breadcrumbs in the blender. Put into a bowl. Put the milk, eggs, Worcestershire sauce, chopped onion, garlic, herbs and seasoning into the blender and blend until the onion is finely chopped. Pour on to the breadcrumbs. Mince the pork finely and add to the breadcrumb mixture. Put into a greased 2lb/1kg loaf tin and bake at 350°F/180°C/Gas Mark 4 for 1 hour. Turn out and serve hot with mushroom or onion sauce (see page 68).

Cold Cheese Mousse

½ *pint/250ml white sauce*
1 *pint/500ml aspic jelly*
3 *tablespoons/45ml salad
   cream*
Salt and pepper
4oz/100g *Cheddar or
   Cheshire cheese*
½ *teaspoon made mustard*
Cucumber slices for garnish

Make up the white sauce (see page 67) and leave to get completely cold. Make up the aspic jelly from crystals and leave to get cold and syrupy. Prepare a soufflé case by tying a stiff band of white paper or of foil round the rim of a soufflé dish, projecting about 2in/5cm above the top. Mix together the white sauce, salad cream, salt and pepper, finely grated cheese and mustard. Whip the aspic jelly until it is just at setting point and foamy and then whip in the cheese mixture with the mixer on low speed until well blended. Put into the prepared soufflé dish and leave in a cold place to set. Remove the paper or foil band and garnish with thin cucumber slices before serving.

Opposite, top: Chicken Liver Pâté (page 33), garnished with olives and served with crisp toast and curls of butter.

Below: Smoked Fish Pâté (page 38), garnished with twists of lemon.

Salmon Mousse

1lb/400g *canned pink salmon*
1oz/25g *butter*
1oz/25g *plain flour*
½ pint/250ml *milk*
Salt and pepper
3 tablespoons/45ml *tomato*
  sauce
1 teaspoon *anchovy essence*
½ teaspoon *lemon juice*
½oz/15g *gelatine*
2 tablespoons/30ml *water*
¼ pint/125ml *double cream*
2 *egg whites*

Prepare a 6in/15cm soufflé dish by tying a band of paper or foil round the outside so that it comes about 2in/5cm above the top of the dish. Drain the salmon and remove skin and bones. Mash the salmon lightly with a fork. Melt the butter, stir in the flour and cook gently for 1 minute. Add the milk and bring to the boil, stirring all the time. Simmer for 3 minutes and season with salt and pepper. Cool slightly and put into the blender with the salmon, tomato sauce, anchovy essence and lemon juice. Stir the gelatine into the water and heat in a bowl over hot water until the gelatine is syrupy. Add to the blender and blend until smooth and creamy. Whip the cream to soft peaks and fold into the salmon mixture. Whisk the egg whites to stiff peaks, fold in the salmon mixture and pour into the soufflé dish. Leave in a cold place until set, and remove the paper collar carefully. The mousse may be garnished with thin slices of cucumber and stuffed olives.

Tongue Mousse

8oz/200g *cooked tongue*
2oz/50g *liver sausage*
3 tablespoons/45ml *thick*
  white sauce
¼ pint/125ml *aspic jelly*
1 teaspoon *gelatine*
¼ pint/125ml *double cream*

Cut the tongue and liver sausage in small pieces and put into the blender with the white sauce. Make up the aspic from crystals and stir in the gelatine. When the aspic is cool and syrupy, pour into the blender and blend until smooth and creamy. Whip the cream to soft peaks and fold in the tongue mixture. Put into a bowl or straight-sided dish rinsed with cold water. Chill and turn out to serve with a green salad.

Chicken Salad Loaf

6oz/150g *cooked chicken*
½oz/15g *gelatine*
¼ pint/125ml *chicken stock or*
  water
Salt and pepper
1 *celery stick*
6 *stuffed olives*
3fl.oz/75ml *mayonnaise*
2oz/50g *cooked peas*

Cut the chicken in very small pieces and put into the blender with the gelatine dissolved in a little water and made up to ¼ pint/125ml with more water or chicken stock. Blend until the chicken is smooth. Season and add the celery and olives. Blend until they are coarsely chopped. Add the mayonnaise and blend until the celery and olives are finely chopped. Fold in the peas and put into a mould rinsed with cold water. Chill until firm, turn out and serve with green salad.

Smoked Haddock Mousse

½ pint/250ml white sauce
12oz/300g smoked haddock
3 tablespoons/45ml
  mayonnaise
Grated rind and juice of ½
  lemon
¼ pint/125ml double cream
½oz/15g gelatine
2 tablespoons/30ml water
Salt and pepper
Watercress and cucumber for
  garnish

Cool the white sauce and put into the blender. Poach the smoked haddock until tender, cool, and break into flakes. Put into the blender with the mayonnaise, grated rind and juice of the lemon, and cream. Dissolve the gelatine in the water over a pan of hot water until the gelatine is syrupy. Cool slightly. Blend the fish mixture until smooth, then pour in the gelatine and seasoning and blend for 10 seconds. Pour into a serving dish. Chill and garnish with watercress sprigs and cucumber slices. For a party finish, make a pattern of cucumber slices on top of the mousse, and add a few peeled shrimps if liked, then pour on a thin layer of cold liquid aspic. Chill until set.

Cheese and Mushroom Loaf

2 medium onions
1 green pepper
1oz/25g butter
4oz/100g mushrooms
4oz/100g brown bread
6oz/150g Cheddar cheese
3 eggs
Salt and pepper
1 tablespoon parsley

Cut the onions and pepper in pieces and chop finely in the blender. Melt the butter and cook the onions and pepper until soft but not browned. Chop the mushrooms coarsely in the blender, add to the butter and continue cooking for 5 minutes. Take off the heat. Make breadcrumbs in the blender and chop the cheese finely in the blender. Put the breadcrumbs and half the cheese into the vegetable mixture with the eggs, seasoning and chopped parsley. Mix very thoroughly and press into a greased loaf tin. Sprinkle with the remaining cheese and bake at 375°F/190°C/Gas Mark 5 for 45 minutes. Turn out on to a hot serving dish, and serve with home-made tomato sauce, or gravy.

Plain Omelette

2 eggs
2 tablespoons/30ml water
Salt and pepper
Butter for frying

Put the eggs, water and seasoning in the blender and blend until well mixed. Melt a knob of butter in a very hot omelette pan and pour in the mixture. Lower the heat and loosen the bottom of the omelette with a palette knife to allow the uncooked mixture to run underneath. As soon as the omelette is set, put in filling, fold and serve on a hot plate. Fillings may be grated cheese, cooked vegetables, mushrooms, ham, asparagus, or creamed poultry, kidneys or fish.

Soufflé Omelette

2 eggs
2 tablespoons/30ml water
Salt and pepper
Butter for frying

Separate the eggs. Mix the water and seasoning with the yolks. Whisk the egg whites on maximum speed to form soft peaks. Gently fold the egg yolks into the whites. Melt some butter in a very hot omelette pan, add the mixture and spread evenly. Cook until almost set and the underneath is golden brown. Put under a hot grill until the omelette is risen and lightly browned. Remove from grill and loosen from pan. Mark across the centre with a knife to aid folding, fill and slip on to a hot plate. Fill soufflé omelettes with grated cheese, cooked mushrooms, chopped ham, asparagus, or creamed ham, chicken or fish.

Spanish Omelette

1 small red pepper
1 small onion
4 medium mushrooms
2 medium tomatoes
1 tablespoon/15ml oil
4 eggs
2 tablespoons/30ml water
Salt and pepper
1oz/25g butter

Remove seeds from the pepper and cut the flesh in pieces. Peel the onion and cut in pieces. Break the mushrooms in pieces and skin the tomatoes. Put the vegetables in the blender and chop coarsely. Cook gently in oil until soft but not coloured. Put the eggs, water and seasoning in the blender, and blend until just mixed. Add the butter to the frying pan, and when it has just melted, pour in the egg mixture. Stir gently and scrape egg from the bottom of the pan. When the eggs are set, but still creamy, do not fold over but serve at once cut in slices and garnished with parsley. If liked, a rasher of bacon and/or chicken liver may be chopped with the vegetables and included in the omelette.

Savoury Soufflés

3 large eggs
2oz/50g plain flour
½ pint/250ml milk
3oz/75g butter
Salt and pepper
Flavourings

Separate the eggs. Put the flour, milk and egg yolks into the blender and blend on low speed until smooth. Melt the butter in a pan and stir in the milk mixture, cooking gently and stirring well until smooth and thick. Take off the heat. Whisk the egg whites to stiff peaks with the mixer and fold into the sauce. Grease a 2 pint/1 litre soufflé dish, fill with mixture and bake at 375°F/190°C/Gas Mark 5 for 45 minutes. Serve and eat at once. This method of cooking gives a crisp crust. For a softer soufflé, stand the dish in a pan of hot but not boiling water in the oven.

Flavourings
Asparagus
Add 6oz/150g cooked or canned asparagus to the cooked sauce, and blend until the asparagus is just chopped before folding in the egg whites.

Cheese
Add 4oz/100g diced Cheddar cheese to milk mixture in the blender with ½ teaspoon mustard powder before cooking the sauce.

Chicken
Add 4oz/100g cooked chicken, a small piece of lemon rind and 1 teaspoon parsley to the cooked sauce, and blend until the chicken is just chopped before folding in the egg whites.

Crab
Add 4oz/100g crabmeat to the sauce, and blend until just mixed before folding in the egg whites.

Danish
Add 6oz/150g chopped cooked bacon, 1oz/25g cheese and a little made mustard to the cooked sauce, and blend until the bacon is finely chopped before folding in the egg whites.

Fish
Add 4oz/100g cooked fish to the sauce, and blend until just mixed before folding in the egg whites. Smoked haddock or kipper are particularly good.

Mushroom
Cook 6oz/150g mushrooms in a little butter, and blend with the cooked sauce until finely chopped before folding in the egg whites.

Seafood
Add 4oz/100g cooked prawns or shrimps and a squeeze of lemon juice to the sauce, and blend until coarsely chopped before folding in the egg whites.

Tomato
Add 4 tablespoons/60ml concentrated tomato purée to the milk mixture before cooking the sauce.

Cheese Crumb Soufflé

3 thick slices white bread
3oz/75g Cheddar cheese
¼ pint/125ml milk
1oz/25g butter
2 eggs
Salt and pepper

Remove the crusts from the bread. Using one slice of bread at a time, tear it into pieces and feed into the blender to make breadcrumbs. Remove the crumbs and continue the process until the bread is used up. Put the crumbs into a bowl. Cut the cheese into small pieces and put them into the blender. Warm the milk and butter until the butter melts. Separate the eggs. Pour the milk and butter into the blender together with the egg yolks and blend until smooth. Pour on to the breadcrumbs, and season with salt and pepper. Whisk the egg whites till stiff but not dry with the mixer. Fold into the cheese mixture, and put into a greased 2 pint/1 litre soufflé dish or pie dish. Bake at 400°F/200°C/Gas Mark 6 for 30 minutes. Serve at once.

Yorkshire Pudding

½ pint/250ml milk
1 egg
½ teaspoon salt
4oz/100g plain flour

Put all the ingredients into the blender, putting in the flour last, and blend until creamy. Pour 3 tablespoons/45ml fat from the roasting joint into a shallow baking tin and heat in the oven until smoking hot. Pour in the batter and bake at 400°F/200°C/Gas Mark 6 for 30 minutes.

Pancakes

½ pint/250ml milk
1 egg
½ teaspoon salt
4oz/100g plain flour

Put all the ingredients into the blender, putting in the flour last, and blend until creamy. Fry thin pancakes in hot fat. Fill with minced meat, creamed chicken, creamed fish or vegetables, roll up pancakes, and top with cheese sauce. Brown under the grill before serving. A light pancake batter may also be made with a mixer whisk.

Fish Puffs

¼ pint/125ml lukewarm
  water
1 tablespoon/15ml oil
4oz/100g plain flour
Pinch of salt
8oz/200g flaked cooked fish
1 tablespoon/15ml lemon
  juice
1oz/25g capers
2 egg whites
Deep fat for frying

Put the water, oil, flour and salt in the blender and blend until thick and creamy. Add the fish, lemon juice and capers and blend until well mixed. Whisk the egg whites with a mixer until stiff and fold into the fish mixture. Put spoonfuls of the mixture into hot fat and cook until the puffs are golden brown and crisp. These are good made with cod, haddock or salmon. They may be served with chips or mashed potatoes and with tomato sauce or chutney.

Savoury Florentine Layer

8 *large thin pancakes*

Tomato filling
8oz/200g *canned tomatoes*
½oz/15g *butter*
1 *medium onion*
½oz/15g *plain flour*
4oz/100g *cooked ham*
Pinch of marjoram
Salt and pepper

Spinach filling
8oz/200g *frozen spinach*
½oz/15g *butter*
¼ *pint/125ml milk*
½oz/15g *cornflour*
Salt and pepper
Pinch of ground nutmeg

Make up the pancakes (see page 58). Prepare the tomato filling by blending the tomatoes with their juice. Melt the butter and cook the chopped onion until soft and golden. Work in the flour and cook for 1 minute. Stir in the tomatoes until the mixture is thickened. Add finely chopped ham, marjoram, salt and pepper and continue cooking for 5 minutes. To make the spinach filling, put the frozen spinach in a pan with the butter, cover and cook gently until thawed. Add the milk and the cornflour blended with a little of the milk. Season with salt, pepper and nutmeg and cook until thickened. Cool slightly and blend the spinach mixture until just smooth. Put one pancake on an ovenware plate, spread on some spinach mixture and top with a second pancake and spread on tomato mixture. Continue in alternating layers and cover with final pancake. Cover lightly with a piece of foil and heat at 375°F/190°C/Gas Mark 5 for 30 minutes. Serve hot, cut in wedges like a cake.

Steak and Kidney Batter

12oz/300g *raw minced beef*
4oz/100g *lamb's or pig's kidneys*
1 *small onion*
2oz/50g *white bread*
1 *teaspoon Worcestershire sauce*
Salt and pepper
½ *pint/250ml Yorkshire Pudding batter*

Put the minced beef into a bowl. Chop the kidneys finely. Chop the onion roughly and put into the blender with pieces of bread. Blend until the onion is finely chopped and the bread is made into crumbs. Add to the meat with the Worcestershire sauce and seasoning and mix well. Form into 8 even-sized balls and put into a greased 7in/17.5cm square tin. Bake at 425°F/220°C/Gas Mark 7 for 15 minutes. Make up the Yorkshire Pudding batter (see page 58) and pour over the meat balls. Bake for 40 minutes until risen and golden. Serve with gravy or tomato sauce.

Beef Fritters

4oz/100g *plain flour*
¼ *teaspoon salt*
1 *egg*
6 *tablespoons/90ml beer*
1*lb*/400g *raw minced beef*
1 *medium onion*
½ *teaspoon mixed herbs*
1 *tablespoon/15ml tomato purée*
1 *tablespoon/15ml French mustard*
Salt and pepper

Make a batter by putting the flour, salt, egg and beer into the blender and blending until thick and creamy (it is best to put the flour into the blender last). Mix together the beef, grated onion, herbs, tomato purée, mustard, salt and pepper very thoroughly and divide into 8 pieces. Shape into balls and press out into thin rounds on a floured surface. Dip into the batter and fry in hot fat or oil for 15 minutes, turning once. Drain well on absorbent paper and serve with tomato sauce. The batter can be made with milk, but beer gives a light crisp fritter.

Plaice Florentine

1*lb*/400g *fresh spinach*
4 *tablespoons/60ml single cream*
2oz/50g *butter*
4 *large plaice fillets*
1oz/25g *Cheddar cheese*
1oz/25g *white bread*
Salt and pepper

Wash the spinach very thoroughly and remove the thick stems. Put into a saucepan with only the water which clings to the stems, cover and cook gently for a minute or two, shaking the pan well so that the spinach cooks without burning. Put the spinach into the blender with any cooking juices, the cream and half the butter. Season lightly and blend until smooth and creamy. Put into a greased shallow ovenware dish and put on the plaice fillets. Cut the cheese in small pieces and break up the bread, and blend together until they are well mixed. Sprinkle the breadcrumbs and cheese on the fish, season with salt and pepper and dot with the remaining butter. Bake at 400°F/200°C/Gas Mark 6 for 20 minutes. Serve very hot.

Kipper Creams

8oz/200g *kipper fillets*
1 *small onion*
3oz/75g *butter*
¼ *pint/125ml white sauce*
2 *teaspoons lemon juice*
2 *teaspoons dry white wine*
Salt and pepper
¼ *pint/125ml double cream*

Put the kipper fillets and coarsely chopped onion into ½ pint/250ml boiling water and poach until the fish is just tender. Break into flakes and remove any skin. Put the kipper flakes, onion, slightly softened butter, white sauce (see page 67), lemon juice, wine and seasoning into the blender and blend until soft and creamy. Pour in the cream and blend just enough to mix well. Put into 4 or 6 individual dishes and chill. If liked, put a thin slice of cucumber on the surface of each kipper cream and cover with a thin layer of aspic jelly.

Quiche Lorraine

8oz/200g shortcrust pastry
1 medium onion
2oz/50g streaky bacon
1oz/25g butter
2 eggs and 2 egg yolks
7fl.oz/175ml creamy milk
Pepper
4oz/100g cheese

Line a flan ring or dish with the pastry. Peel the onion and cut it in pieces. Remove the rind from the bacon and cut the bacon in pieces. Chop the onion and bacon finely in the blender, and cook until soft in the butter. Put into the bottom of the pastry case. Put the eggs, egg yolks, milk and pepper in the blender together with the cheese cut in small pieces. Blend so that the eggs and milk are well mixed together. Pour into the flan case. Bake at 375°F/190°C/Gas Mark 5 for 35 minutes. Serve hot or cold.

Ratatouille Flan

8oz/200g shortcrust pastry
4oz/100g aubergine
4oz/100g tomatoes
1 small onion
1 small green pepper
4oz/100g streaky bacon
2oz/50g butter
Salt and pepper
4oz/100g Cheddar cheese

Roll out the pastry and line an 8in/20cm flan ring or tin. Cut the aubergine in pieces. Skin tomatoes and remove the pips. Peel the onion and cut in pieces, and remove the seeds from the green pepper. Cut the bacon in pieces. Put the vegetables and bacon in the blender and blend until roughly chopped. Cook gently in the butter until the vegetables are soft but not coloured. Season with salt and pepper and leave until cold. Put into the pastry case. Cut the cheese in pieces and blend in small quantities until finely chopped. Bake the filled flan at 400°F/200°C/Gas Mark 6 for 30 minutes. Spread the cheese on top of the vegetables and continue baking for 15 minutes until the cheese has melted and is golden-brown. Serve hot.

Spanish Olive Flan

8oz/200g shortcrust pastry
2oz/75g streaky bacon
½ small green pepper
4oz/100g Cheddar cheese
10 stuffed green olives
2 eggs
¼ pint/125ml single cream
Salt and pepper

Roll out the pastry and line an 8in/20cm flan ring or tin. Bake blind at 400°F/200°C/Gas Mark 6 for 15 minutes. Cut the bacon in pieces and cook gently until the fat runs and the bacon is soft. Put into the blender with the fat and green pepper and blend until finely chopped. Spread on the base of the pastry. Cut the cheese in pieces and blend in small quantities until finely chopped. Sprinkle the cheese on to the bacon and green pepper. Cut the olives in half and put on the cheese. Put the eggs, cream, salt and pepper into the blender and blend until well mixed. Pour into the pastry case and bake at 350°F/180°C/Gas Mark 4 for 25 minutes. Serve hot or cold.

Smoked Haddock Flan

6oz/150g shortcrust pastry
1 *small onion*
2oz/50g streaky bacon
1oz/25g butter
6oz/150g *cooked smoked
    haddock*
2 eggs
6fl.oz/150ml milk
Salt and pepper

Line a 6in/15cm flan ring with the pastry. Cut the onion and bacon in pieces and chop finely in the blender. Cook in the butter until soft but not coloured. Spread in the base of the pastry case. Put the cooked haddock, eggs, milk and seasoning in the blender, and blend until the fish is broken into small pieces. Pour into the flan case and bake at 375°F/190°C/Gas Mark 5 for 45 minutes. A few shrimps or prawns may be added to the filling, or a little grated cheese may be sprinkled on top before baking.

Chicken Vol-au-vents

12 *vol-au-vent cases*
1oz/25g butter
1oz/25g *plain flour*
¼ pint/125ml chicken stock
¼ pint/125ml milk
8oz/200g cooked chicken
1 *small green pepper*
2 tablespoons/30ml single
    cream
½ teaspoon/2.5ml Tabasco
    pepper sauce
Salt and pepper

Bake the vol-au-vent cases. Melt the butter. Put the flour, chicken stock and milk in the blender and blend until smooth. Pour on to the butter and stir over a gentle heat until the mixture boils. Simmer for 2 minutes, stirring well. Return to the blender with the chicken cut in pieces, green pepper, cream, Tabasco sauce, salt and pepper, and blend until the chicken is finely chopped. Return to saucepan and simmer for 8 minutes. Fill the vol-au-vent cases and serve hot. If liked, a few mushrooms may be added to the mixture, or ham or seafood may be substituted for the chicken.

Pizza

½oz/15g fresh yeast
8oz/200g plain flour
8 *medium tomatoes*
Salt and pepper
12 anchovy fillets
6oz/150g cheese
2 teaspoons marjoram
Olive oil

Dissolve the yeast in a little tepid water and put into the flour, salting well. Mix with the dough hook of a mixer, adding a little more warm water to make a stiff dough. When the dough is smooth and shiny, form into a ball, cover with a cloth and leave in a warm place to rise for about 2 hours until double in volume. Roll out in two 7in/18cm circles about ¼in/6mm thick. Skin the tomatoes, remove pips, and chop the flesh. Spread on the dough, seasoning well with salt and pepper. Arrange anchovy fillets on top with thin slices of cheese, and sprinkle with marjoram and a little olive oil. Bake at 425°F/220°C/Gas Mark 7 for 30 minutes. The best cheese to use is Mozzarella, but Bel Paese or Cheddar can be substituted. Black olives may also be added to the topping. For a variation, use a topping of onion/ham/pepper, or salami/mushrooms/cheese.

Devilled Sausages

1lb/400g pork sausages
1oz/25g butter
1 medium onion
1oz/25g plain flour
¼ pint/125ml water
2 tablespoons/30ml sweet
  pickle
2 teaspoons Worcestershire
  sauce
2 tablespoons/30ml tomato
  sauce
1 teaspoon made mustard
1 tablespoon/15ml vinegar
½ teaspoon salt

Grill the sausages until lightly browned. Melt the butter and cook the finely chopped onion until soft and golden. Stir in the flour and cook for 2 minutes. Add to the water and bring to the boil. Cool slightly and put into the blender with the pickle, sauces, mustard, vinegar and salt. Blend until smooth and pour over the sausages in a thick saucepan. Cover and simmer for 30 minutes. Serve very hot with mashed potatoes.

Cheese Pudding

2 eggs
½ pint milk
3oz/75g Cheshire cheese
2oz/50g white bread
½ teaspoon mustard powder
½ teaspoon salt
2 tablespoons parsley

Separate the eggs. Put the egg yolks and lukewarm milk into the blender and blend until creamy. Pour over the grated cheese. Break the bread into pieces and make into breadcrumbs in the blender, adding mustard, salt and parsley during the final blending. Add to the cheese mixture and leave to stand for 30 minutes. Whisk the egg whites to stiff peaks and fold into the mixture. Pour into a greased ovenware dish and bake at 400°F/200°C/Gas Mark 6 for 30 minutes.

Cream Cheese Rolls

6oz/150g full fat soft cheese
Grated rind of ½ lemon
½ teaspoon Worcestershire
  sauce
3 tablespoons/45ml milk
1 teaspoon mixed herbs
6 slices ham or roast beef

Cut the cheese into pieces and put into the blender with the lemon rind, Worcestershire sauce, milk and herbs. Blend until smooth and creamy. Spread on the ham or beef and roll up lightly. Serve with salad.

Apple and Walnut Salad

1 small crisp lettuce
6 sticks celery
3 eating apples
3oz/75g walnuts
¼ pint/125ml mayonnaise
5 tablespoons/75ml double
  cream

Wash the lettuce, shake dry and break into pieces. Arrange in a serving bowl. Cut the celery into pieces. Without peeling the apples, remove the cores and cut the apples into pieces. Put celery, apples and walnuts into the blender and blend until coarsely chopped. Stir the mayonnaise and double cream together and mix into the apple mixture. Arrange on lettuce leaves.

Meat Croquettes

8oz/200g cooked meat or
  poultry
1 small onion
½ teaspoon mixed herbs
1 teaspoon parsley
½oz/15g dripping
½oz/15g plain flour
¼ pint/125ml stock
Salt and pepper

Cut the meat or poultry into pieces. Peel the onion and cut it into pieces. Put the meat, onion, mixed herbs and parsley into the blender and chop finely. Melt the dripping, work in the flour and then the stock and cook until smooth and thick. Stir in the meat mixture and season with salt and pepper. Cook for 3 minutes, then cool completely by flattening the mixture out on a plate. Shape into flat cakes or sausage shapes and coat with a little beaten egg and some dry breadcrumbs (these can be made in the blender). Fry until golden brown and drain well. Serve with gravy, barbecue or tomato sauce and vegetables.

Fish croquettes

Fish croquettes may be made in a similar way, making the sauce with butter and milk instead of dripping and flour. Add a little tomato sauce for extra flavouring and a couple of hard-boiled eggs chopped in with the fish.

Fish Cakes

1lb/400g cooked fish
2 large eggs
1oz/25g plain flour
2 tablespoons/30ml lemon
  juice
2 tablespoons parsley
1 teaspoon/5ml
  Worcestershire sauce
1½oz/40g melted butter
Salt and pepper
1lb/400g mashed potatoes

Break fish into small pieces and put into the blender with the eggs, flour, lemon juice, parsley, Worcestershire sauce, butter and seasoning. Cover and blend until fish is well broken up. Work mixture into mashed potatoes. Divide into 16 pieces and make into round flat cakes. Coat with beaten egg and breadcrumbs, and fry until golden. These are usually made with cod or haddock, but they are especially good made with smoked haddock, kippers, or drained canned salmon.

Pork Sausages

4oz/100g stale bread
1½lb/600g lean and fat pork
1 egg
1 teaspoon mixed herbs
Salt and pepper
Sausage skins (optional)

Soak the bread in water and squeeze out the excess moisture. Put into a mixing bowl. Mince the meat finely. Mix with the bread, egg and seasoning, using the heavy beater of the mixer until the ingredients are well blended together. The mixture may now be chilled slightly, then formed into sausage shapes and fried. The sausages may be coated with flour, egg and breadcrumbs if liked. If sausage skins are preferred, buy these from the butcher, and use the sausage-filling attachment on the mincer.

Golden Salad

4 medium carrots
2oz/50g salted peanuts
Mayonnaise
Green salad
4 pineapple rings

Shred the carrots and peanuts coarsely and mix with enough mayonnaise to moisten. Put the green salad on to plates, top with pineapple rings and then the carrot and nut mixture.

Coleslaw

½ white cabbage
4 sticks celery
3 medium carrots
½ small onion
Pinch of salt
Sour Cream Dressing (see page 75)

Slice the cabbage and celery finely and shred the carrots and onion coarsely. Stir in a little salt, then toss in Sour Cream Dressing just before serving. A few seedless raisins may be added, or some nut kernels.

Health Salad

2 red-skinned apples
2 sticks celery
Juice of ½ lemon
2oz/50g walnuts
2oz/50g seedless raisins
Mayonnaise
Lettuce leaves

Wipe the apples and clean the celery. Shred the apples and celery and put into a bowl. Toss in lemon juice at once to prevent fruit turning brown. Stir in walnuts and raisins with mayonnaise to moisten and serve on a bed of lettuce leaves.

7 Savoury Sauces and Stuffings

Good sauces and stuffings can help to add interest to otherwise simple meals, and the blender is invaluable for making both. Once the basic technique is mastered, a little imagination can be added to vary recipes to suit family requirements, by the addition of favourite herbs or other flavourings.

Sauces

When making sauces, the ingredients must be carefully weighed, cooked correctly and smoothed to perfection. With a blender, raw ingredients may be mixed before cooking, and this can be particularly useful if preparing a sauce in which meat, poultry or fish is to be casseroled as the finely processed ingredients will release all their flavours. When preparing the initial blend of raw ingredients, it is important to put liquid into the blender first, and then add flour and more solid ingredients. For a smooth sauce to serve as a coating (e.g. white sauce), the sauce may be returned to a blender after cooking, and blended again until smooth. This smoothing may slightly thin the sauce, and overblending must be avoided.

Many people avoid making the sauces with a tricky reputation such as Mayonnaise or Hollandaise, but these give no problem with a blender because ingredients can be added slowly through the hole in the lid while the motor is running. Mayonnaise can also be made successfully with a mixer which is running, as oil can be put in very slowly with a dropper or poured in slowly from a jug.

Stuffings

Stuffings are most useful in the kitchen, for not only do they add flavour and interest to many foods, but they also help to extend servings of expensive meat, poultry or fish, or make cheaper meat more appetizing. It is best to use day-old bread for stuffing, which will be slightly easier to make into crumbs and which will also produce a better-textured stuffing. Onions, herbs, hard-boiled eggs, nuts and dried fruit can also be chopped in the blender to add to the stuffing.

The complete stuffing may be made in the blender, starting with the breadcrumbs in a dry goblet. Only process small quantities at a time, as it is better to make two or three quantities rather than overloading the machine. Herbs are strengthened in flavour by being finely chopped in the blender, so use them with care. Don't add too much liquid to a stuffing in the form of eggs, stock or water as a stuffing should be dry and crumbly when put into the food. It will absorb juices from meat, poultry and fish during the cooking process, and if it is already wet, the result will be stodgy and heavy.

Apple Sauce

1lb/400g cooking apples
4 tablespoons/60ml water
Sugar
1oz/25g butter

Wash the apples and remove the cores, but do not peel them. Cut in pieces and put into a pan with the water. Simmer until soft, and add sugar to taste (to serve with meat or poultry, the sauce should not be too sweet). Put into the blender with the butter and blend on medium speed until smooth.

Barbecue Sauce

1 medium onion
1oz/25g butter
½oz/15g plain flour
2 teaspoons/10ml French
 mustard
½ teaspoon dry mustard
1 tablespoon/15ml
 Worcestershire sauce
1 teaspoon/5ml Tabasco
 sauce
½oz/15g brown sugar
1 teaspoon salt
1 tablespoon/15ml vinegar
8fl.oz/200ml tomato juice

Peel the onion, cut it into pieces, and chop finely in the blender. Cook in the butter until golden. Stir in the flour and cook for 2 minutes. Put into the blender with the remaining ingredients, and blend until smooth. Bring to boiling point and then simmer for 5 minutes, stirring well.

Basic White Sauce

½ pint/250ml milk
1oz/25g plain flour
1oz/25g butter
Salt and pepper

Put the milk and flour into the blender. Cover and blend until smooth. Melt the butter and pour on the mixture from the blender. Stir over a gentle heat until the mixture boils, and then simmer for 2 minutes, stirring well. Season to taste. For a very smooth sauce, return to blender, cover and blend on medium speed for 10 seconds.

Parsley Sauce
Blend 1 tablespoon fresh parsley with the milk and flour.

Onion Sauce
Chop 1 large onion in the blender and cook in the butter before adding the milk and flour mixture.

Egg Sauce
Blend the cooked sauce with 2 hard-boiled eggs.

Cheese Sauce
Cut 3oz/75g cheese in pieces and put in the blender. Cover and blend on medium speed for 10 seconds. Add to the white sauce and cook until just melted, seasoning with a little mustard.

Caper Sauce
Blend 2oz/50g capers with the milk and flour.

Mushroom Sauce
Chop 3oz/75g mushrooms in blender and soften in butter before adding the milk and flour mixture.

Bread Sauce

2 cloves
1 small onion
½ pint/250ml milk
3oz/75g white bread
1oz/25g butter
Salt and pepper
2 tablespoons/30ml single cream

Stick the cloves into the onion, and put it into a thick pan with the milk. Bring just to boiling point and then leave in a warm place for 30 minutes. Remove the onion, and put the milk into the blender with the bread broken into small pieces. Blend on low speed until smooth. Return to the saucepan with the butter, salt and pepper and reheat. Just before serving, stir in the cream.

Brown Sauce

1 onion
1 carrot
½oz/15g butter
½ pint/250ml brown stock
Salt and pepper
½oz/15g plain flour

Cut the onion and carrot in pieces and then chop finely in the blender. Melt the butter and cook the vegetables until soft but not coloured. Add the stock, salt and pepper and simmer for 30 minutes. Return to the blender with the flour and blend until smooth. Bring to the boil, stirring well and cook for 3 minutes.

Curry Sauce

2oz/50g lard or dripping
1 medium onion
1oz/25g plain flour
½oz/12g curry powder
¾ pint/375ml stock
1 apple
2oz/50g sultanas
2 teaspoons/10ml lemon juice
Salt and pepper
Pinch of caster sugar

Melt the lard or dripping. Chop the onion finely in the blender and cook in the fat until lightly golden and soft. Add the flour and curry powder and cook for 3 minutes. Put the stock in the blender with the apple and blend until the apple is finely chopped. Stir this mixture into the onion mixture and simmer for 10 minutes. Add the sultanas, lemon juice, salt and pepper and sugar and simmer for 2 minutes. Use this sauce with hard-boiled eggs, seafood, cooked chicken or meat. If a completely smooth sauce is preferred, blend the sauce after the final cooking and reheat for 3 minutes.

Chutney Sauce

3 tablespoons/45ml spicy bottled sauce
1 tablespoon/15ml concentrated tomato purée
5fl.oz/125ml apple purée
2 eating apples
1 banana
½oz/15g almond kernels
½oz/15g walnut kernels
2oz/50g raisins

Put the bottled sauce, tomato purée and apple purée into the blender. Peel and core the apples and cut them in rough pieces. Peel the banana and cut in pieces. Put into the blender with the nuts and blend until the nuts are finely chopped. Mix with the raisins and serve hot or cold with meat, poultry or fish.

Hollandaise Sauce

4oz/100g unsalted butter
3 egg yolks
1 tablespoon/15ml lemon juice
1 tablespoon/15ml tepid water
Salt and pepper

Heat the butter until melted but not brown. Put the egg yolks, lemon juice, water and seasonings into the blender. Cover and blend on low speed for 5 seconds. While the blender is running, start to pour the warm butter gently through the centre section of the cover. Continue blending until the sauce has thickened and then switch off immediately. Serve at once with fish, especially salmon, and with vegetables. This sauce is particularly good with asparagus and artichokes.

Aurora Sauce
Fold 3 tablespoons/45ml mayonnaise and ¼ pint/125ml whipped cream into Hollandaise Sauce and serve with cold chicken or fish.

Maltaise Sauce
Stir in 1 tablespoon/15ml orange juice and 1 teaspoon grated orange rind, and serve with vegetables.

Mousseline Sauce
Stir $\frac{1}{4}$ pint/125ml whipped cream into sauce and serve with fish, eggs or vegetables.

Horseradish Cream Sauce

$\frac{1}{4}$ pint/125ml double cream
1 tablespoon/15ml lemon
  juice
1 teaspoon/5ml horseradish
  sauce
2 teaspoons/10ml
  Worcestershire sauce
2 spring onions

Put cream, lemon juice, horseradish sauce and Worcestershire sauce into the blender. Cut the white part and a little of the green of the onions into pieces and add to the blender. Blend until the onions are very finely chopped. Chill and serve with steak, roast beef, beef-burgers, or jacket potatoes.

Indonesian Sauce

1 tablespoon/15ml salad oil
4 tablespoons/60ml peanut
  butter
$\frac{1}{4}$ pint/125ml tomato sauce
3 tablespoons/45ml
  Worcestershire sauce
1 garlic clove
Large pinch of salt

Heat the oil gently in a pan and stir in the peanut butter. Continue heating gently, stirring occasionally, until the peanut butter begins to thicken and darken slightly. Put into the blender with all the other ingredients. Blend until smooth and leave to stand for 2 hours before using. Reheat gently and serve with chicken, steak or kebabs. If the sauce is rather thick, blend in a little water before reheating.

Mint Sauce

$\frac{1}{4}$ pint/125ml vinegar
4 heaped tablespoons mint
  leaves
2 tablespoons/30ml boiling
  water
$\frac{1}{2}$oz/15g sugar
Pinch of salt

Put all the ingredients into the blender, and blend until the mint is finely chopped. Cool before serving.

Rich Mushroom Sauce

1 *medium onion*
½*oz/15g butter*
6*oz/150g mushrooms*
¼ *pint/125ml red wine*
¼ *pint/125ml beef stock*
½*oz/15g cornflour*
1 *tablespoon/15ml*
   Worcestershire sauce
Salt and pepper

Cut the onion in pieces and then chop it finely in the butter. Fry the onion until soft in the butter. Cut the mushrooms in pieces and put into the blender with the wine and stock. Blend until the mushrooms are finely chopped. Return to the saucepan and simmer for 10 minutes. Pour some of the sauce into the blender and add the cornflour, Worcestershire sauce, salt and pepper, and blend until smooth. Return to the pan with the remaining sauce, and simmer for 5 minutes. This sauce is very good with roast beef or steak, and with poultry.

Sweet and Sour Sauce

1½*oz/40g sugar*
½*oz/15g cornflour*
2 *teaspoons/10ml soya sauce*
2 *tablespoons/30ml vinegar*
2 *teaspoons/10ml concen-*
   trated tomato purée
Pinch of salt
½ *pint/250ml water*
3*oz/75g drained canned*
   pineapple
1 *small onion*

Put sugar, cornflour, soya sauce, vinegar, tomato purée, salt and water into the blender, and blend for 30 seconds until smooth. Put into a saucepan and simmer gently until the sauce thickens, stirring well. Put the pineapple and quartered onion in the blender with a little of the sauce, and blend until the pineapple and onion are finely chopped. Return to the pan with the remaining sauce and simmer for 3 minutes.

Tomato Sauce

1 *medium onion*
1 *garlic clove*
1 *tablespoon/15ml olive oil*
1*lb/400g ripe tomatoes*
1 *teaspoon salt*
1 *teaspoon sugar*
1 *teaspoon paprika*
1 *tablespoon/15ml vinegar*
1 *bay leaf*
Pepper

Peel the onion and cut it into pieces. Chop finely in the blender with the garlic clove. Cook gently in the oil until golden. Skin the tomatoes and chop them coarsely in the blender. Add to the onion with all the other ingredients and simmer for 15 minutes. Take out the bay leaf and blend the sauce on medium speed until smooth. Put through a sieve and simmer for 20 minutes.

Tomato Barbecue Sauce

4lb/2kg ripe tomatoes
1oz/25g salt
8oz/200g sugar
½ teaspoon Cayenne pepper
1oz/25g ground ginger
2 garlic cloves
1½ teaspoons mustard powder

Cut up the tomatoes and put into a pan with the salt, sugar, pepper, ginger, chopped garlic and mustard. Bring to the boil and simmer until the mixture has reduced to half, which will take about an hour. Stir often to prevent burning. Either blend and then sieve, or use a colander-and-sieve attachment on the mixer. Reheat the sauce just to boiling point, pour into hot preserving jars or sauce bottles and seal.

Sweet Devil Sauce

3oz/75g soft brown sugar
3 tablespoons/45ml vinegar
1 tablespoon/15ml olive oil
1 garlic clove
1½oz/40g mustard powder
Pinch of salt

Put the sugar into the blender. Heat the vinegar and add to the blender with the oil, chopped garlic, mustard powder and salt. Blend until smooth and creamy. Put into a bowl, cover and leave to stand for 24 hours before using with boiled beef, tongue or ham.

Cranberry Apple Sauce

1lb/400g cranberries
1lb/400g cooking apples
1 pint/500ml water
6oz/150g sugar

Put the cranberries and the peeled and cored apples into the blender in small quantities with the water and blend until finely chopped. Add the sugar and simmer over low heat until the fruit is soft. Return to the blender and blend until smooth. Serve with pork or turkey.

Salad Cream

¾ pint/375ml milk
1½oz/40g plain flour
1½oz/40g sugar
2 teaspoons mustard powder
2oz/50g margarine
1 egg
¼ pint/125ml vinegar

Put the milk into the blender with the flour and blend until smooth, then blend in the sugar and mustard powder. Melt the margarine and pour in the liquid. Stir over low heat until thick and creamy. Cool and put into the blender with the egg. Blend until creamy and gradually add the vinegar through the hole in the lid with the motor running, until it is all absorbed. This will keep for 4 weeks in a cold place.

Mixer Mayonnaise

2 egg yolks
½ teaspoon salt
½ teaspoon mustard powder
¼ teaspoon pepper
½ pint/250ml olive oil
1 tablespoon/15ml lemon
  juice or vinegar

Put the egg yolks with salt, mustard and pepper into the mixer bowl and whisk on maximum speed for 10 seconds. Drop in the olive oil very slowly, with the mixer running, until nearly all the oil has been completely absorbed. Add the lemon juice or vinegar and continue whisking until all the oil has been absorbed.

Green Mayonnaise
Chop 1 garlic clove, 1 tablespoon fresh dill, 1 tablespoon fresh chives and 1 tablespoon fresh parsley in the blender and add to the mayonnaise. Use for tomatoes, cucumbers or fish.

Green Goddess Mayonnaise
Use tarragon vinegar for the mayonnaise. Chop 1 garlic clove, 2 anchovy fillets, 3 spring onions (including green tops) and 2 tablespoons parsley in the blender and add to the mayonnaise. Use for seafood.

Tomato Mayonnaise
Cut up 1 small green pepper, and put into the blender with 2 tablespoons/30ml tomato purée, 1 teaspoon tarragon and 1 table-spoon chives. Blend on high speed for 5 seconds before adding to the mayonnaise. Use for seafood.

Cucumber Mayonnaise
Cut up ¼ cucumber (including the skin) and put into the blender with 1 slice of onion, and 2 teaspoons/10ml mild made mustard, with salt and pepper. Blend on high speed for 5 seconds until the cucumber is finely chopped. Add 3 tablespoons/45ml mayonnaise and blend until just mixed. Serve with fish, poultry or ham.

Blender Mayonnaise

1 standard egg
1 tablespoon/15ml vinegar or
  lemon juice
½ teaspoon salt
1 teaspoon sugar
¼ teaspoon dry mustard
¼ teaspoon pepper
½ pint/250ml salad oil

Put the egg, vinegar or lemon juice, salt, sugar, mustard and pepper into the blender. Cover and blend on medium speed for 5 seconds. Start to pour the oil gently through the centre section of the cover while the blender is running. Continue blending for about 1 minute until the oil has been incorporated. It may be necessary to stop the blender and scrape down the sides with a spatula. This gives a creamy mixture, but if a thicker mayonnaise is preferred, use two egg yolks instead of the whole egg.

Tartare Sauce

Mayonnaise
8 sprigs parsley
6 gherkins
6 stuffed olives
2 pickled onions
2 teaspoons capers

Make the mayonnaise as in the previous recipe, and during the last stage of thickening, add the other ingredients until coarsely chopped. Serve with fish.

Salad Dressing

1 teaspoon dry mustard
1 teaspoon salt
½ teaspoon black pepper
¼oz/6g caster sugar
½ pint/250ml salad or olive oil
¼ pint/125ml wine vinegar

Put all the ingredients into the blender and blend on high speed. Dress salad just before serving, or serve in a bowl.

Blue Cheese Dressing

4oz/100g cottage cheese
2oz/50g blue cheese
3 tablespoons/45ml salad cream
2 tablespoons/30ml top milk
1 teaspoon/5ml made mustard
2 teaspoons/10ml lemon juice
1 teaspoon chives

Put all the ingredients into the blender and blend until smooth. Chill and serve on crisp lettuce hearts.

Devil Dressing

1 orange
1 tablespoon/15ml made mustard
2 tablespoons/30ml red-currant jelly
1 tablespoon grated horseradish

Squeeze the juice from the orange and put into the blender with one thin slice of orange peel without pith. Add the other ingredients and blend until the peel is very finely chopped. Simmer for 3 minutes and serve hot or cold with ham or pork.

Low-Calorie Dressing

4 tablespoons/60ml tomato
  juice
1 thin slice onion
1 teaspoon/5ml made
  mustard
Salt and pepper
1 tablespoon parsley or mint

Instead of tomato juice, a mixture of orange and lemon juice, or orange and grapefruit juice may be used. Put all the ingredients into the blender and blend until the onion and herbs are finely chopped. Use with green salads or vegetable salads.

Sour Cream Dressing

8 fl.oz/200ml soured cream
2 tablespoons/30ml vinegar
1 tablespoon/15ml lemon
  juice
½ teaspoon salt
1½oz/40g sugar
Pepper

Put all the ingredients into the mixer bowl and mix on minimum speed until creamy and well blended. Serve cold with seafood or salads.

Yogurt Salad Dressing

¼ pint/125ml natural yogurt
1 teaspoon parsley
1 teaspoon chives
1 thin slice onion
1 teaspoon/5ml made
  mustard

Put the yogurt, herbs, onion and mustard into the blender, and blend until the herbs are finely chopped. Serve cold with salads or fish. A thick slice of cucumber may be added if liked (including the skin).

Poultry Marinade

2 carrots
2 onions
2 garlic cloves
4 tablespoons/60ml olive oil
Salt and pepper
Sprig of thyme
Sprig of parsley
1 bay leaf
8 fl.oz/200ml white wine

Cut the carrots and onions in pieces and put into the blender with the garlic. Blend until chopped finely, and then cook in the oil until lightly browned. Put into the blender with the seasoning and herbs (except bay leaf) and water to cover. Blend until smooth, add bay leaf, and then simmer for 10 minutes. Add the wine, bring to the boil and then cool before using. Remove the bay leaf and pour over poultry pieces and leave overnight in a cold place. Drain the poultry before using. Use the marinade in your recipe to give added flavour.

Red Meat Marinade

4fl.oz/100ml dry white wine
4fl.oz/100ml wine vinegar
4fl.oz/100ml olive oil
1 small onion
1 small carrot
Thyme, parsley and bay leaf
2 garlic cloves
Salt and pepper
4 whole cloves

Put all the ingredients except the cloves into the blender, and blend until the vegetables are chopped finely. Add the cloves and pour over red meat. Leave in a cold place overnight. Drain the meat before using, but use the marinade in the recipe to give added flavour. This marinade is also good for pigeon, hare, venison and other game.

Herb Marinade

4fl.oz/100ml olive or salad
  oil
2fl.oz/50ml lemon juice
½ teaspoon salt
¼ teaspoon pepper
½ teaspoon marjoram
½ teaspoon thyme
½ teaspoon rosemary
2 tablespoons parsley
1 garlic clove
1 medium onion

Put all the ingredients into the blender, with the onion cut into pieces. Blend until the onion is finely chopped. Pour over lamb or chicken and leave in a cold place overnight. Drain the meat before using, but add the marinade to the recipe if stewing, or brush the meat with marinade while grilling. This is a very good marinade to use with kebabs, or with barbecued chicken pieces.

Basic Poultry Stuffing

1 small loaf day-old bread
1 medium onion
3 tablespoons parsley
1 tablespoon thyme
2oz/50g melted butter
Salt and pepper
1 teaspoon/5ml lemon juice

Cut the bread into small pieces and blend in small quantities to make fine breadcrumbs. Put the crumbs into a bowl. Cut the onion in pieces and put into the blender with the remaining ingredients. Blend until the herbs are finely chopped. Pour on to the breadcrumbs and stir until well mixed. This is enough for a bird weighing 4lb/2kg. An egg may be added for a more solid stuffing.

Giblet Stuffing
The giblets of the bird may be cooked, and the liver, heart and meat from the neck added to the herbs and butter to be finely chopped before adding to the breadcrumbs.

Raisin and Nut Stuffing
Chop 4oz/100g walnut halves and 6oz/150g seedless raisins in the blender and add to the other ingredients. Use for poultry or pork.

Opposite, from top left to right: Lamb in Cider (page 45), boned and rolled shoulder with Mushroom Stuffing (page 81), and leg of lamb with Apricot Stuffing (page 81).

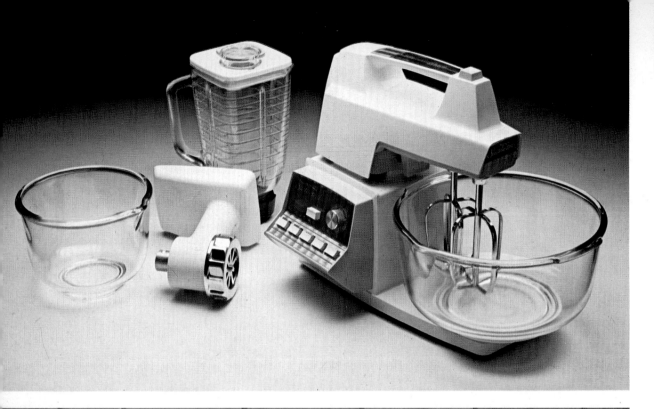

Sweet and Sour Marinade

4 *tablespoons/60ml pineapple
  juice*
1 *tablespoon/15ml soy sauce*
1 *tablespoon/15ml lemon
  juice*
1 *garlic clove*
Salt

Put all the ingredients into the blender and blend until the garlic is finely crushed. Pour over lean pork or lamb or chicken joints and leave in a cold place for 2 hours, turning the meat often. Grill the meat or poultry, basting frequently with the marinade.

Beer Marinade

½ *pint/250ml beer*
6 *tablespoons/90ml oil*
1 *garlic clove*
2 *tablespoons/30ml lemon
  juice*
1oz/25g *sugar*
½ *teaspoon salt*

Put all the ingredients into the blender and blend until the garlic is finely crushed. Pour over meat or game, cover and leave in a cold place for 5 hours, turning at least once. Use for beef or game and include the marinade in your recipe to give added flavour. If used for steaks, drain the meat before grilling, but baste the meat with the marinade during cooking.

Cider Marinade

6 *tablespoons/90ml dry cider*
3 *tablespoons/45ml oil*
1 *garlic clove*
1 *small onion*
Salt and pepper
½ *teaspoon rosemary or thyme*

Put all the ingredients into the blender and blend until the onion is finely chopped. Pour over chicken joints, cover and leave for 3 hours, turning the chicken at least twice. Grill the chicken joints, basting with the marinade during cooking.

Apple and Walnut Stuffing

1lb/400g *cooking apples*
1oz/25g *walnuts*
1oz/25g *sugar*
4oz/100g *white bread*
1 *small onion*
1 *teaspoon salt*
Pepper
1 *egg*
2oz/50g *butter*

Peel and core the apples, cut into pieces and put into the blender with the walnuts. Blend until finely chopped. Remove from the blender and put into a bowl with the sugar. Break the bread into small pieces and make into breadcrumbs in the blender, adding the onion during final blending until it is finely chopped. Add to the apple and work in the salt and pepper, egg and melted butter. Use for pork, duck, goose or bacon joints.

Opposite, top: A kitchen centre (Sunbeam) with blender, mixer and mincer attachments.

Below: The Kenwood Mini with its stand and bowl.

Celery and Tomato Stuffing

4oz/100g *white bread*
1 *celery stick*
2 *tomatoes*
1oz/25g *butter*
4 *tablespoons/60ml milk*
½ *teaspoon salt*

Break the bread into pieces and make into crumbs in the blender. Put into a bowl. Cut the celery in pieces. Peel the tomatoes, remove the pips and cut the flesh into pieces. Warm the butter and milk together until the butter melts. Put the celery, tomatoes, salt, butter and milk into the blender, and blend until the celery is finely chopped. Pour on to the breadcrumbs and mix well. Use for stuffing lamb, veal, poultry or fish.

Bacon Stuffing

4oz/100g *white bread*
4oz/100g *lean bacon*
½ *teaspoon mustard powder*
¼ *teaspoon salt*
½ *teaspoon mixed herbs*
1oz/25g *butter*
4 *tablespoons/60ml milk*

Break the bread into pieces and cut the bacon into small pieces. Make breadcrumbs in the blender adding the bacon gradually until it is chopped finely. Add the mustard, salt and herbs during the final blending. Put into a bowl. Melt the butter and milk together and pour on to the breadcrumbs. Mix well. Use for stuffing chicken, turkey or veal.

Pineapple Stuffing

4oz/100g *white bread*
2oz/50g *cooked lean ham*
4 *pineapple chunks*
1 *small onion*
Salt and pepper
1oz/25g *butter*
4 *tablespoons/60ml milk*

Break the bread into small pieces and make into breadcrumbs in the blender. During the final blending, add the ham, pineapple and onion cut in pieces, and blend until they are finely chopped. Put into a bowl, season with salt and pepper and stir in the butter and milk heated together. Use with pork or poultry.

Prawn Stuffing

4oz/100g *white bread*
1 *tablespoon parsley*
½ *teaspoon grated lemon rind*
2oz/50g *peeled prawns*
Salt and pepper
1oz/25g *butter*
4 *tablespoons/60ml milk*

Break the bread into small pieces and make into breadcrumbs in the blender. Add the parsley, lemon rind and prawns during the final blending and blend until the prawns are roughly chopped. Put into a bowl and add the seasoning and the butter and milk heated together. Mix well. Use for fish or tomatoes.

Apricot Stuffing

4oz/100g dried apricots
8oz/200g day-old bread
2 sticks celery
2oz/50g melted butter
Salt and pepper

Cover the apricots with water, bring to the boil and simmer for 5 minutes. Break the bread into pieces and blend in small quantities to make breadcrumbs. Put into a mixing bowl. Put the apricots and cooking liquid into the blender with the celery, and blend until the fruit and celery are coarsely chopped. Pour on to the breadcrumbs and mix with the melted butter and seasoning. Use for chicken, duck or pork.

Chestnut Stuffing

1lb/400g chestnuts
Milk
2oz/50g day-old bread
1oz/25g melted butter
2 teaspoons fresh mixed herbs
2 eggs
Salt and pepper
Pinch of mustard powder

Split the chestnuts and boil them in water for 10 minutes. Take off the skins and put the chestnuts in just enough milk to cover. Simmer until tender. Put into the blender with the milk and blend until finely chopped. Add the bread in small pieces, butter, herbs, eggs and seasoning, and blend until well mixed. Use for chicken or turkey, but double the quantity for a large turkey.

Prune Stuffing

1lb/400g prunes
Red wine
1 lemon
8oz/200g fresh pork
1 small onion
12 green olives, stoned
2oz/50g butter
Salt and pepper
Pinch of nutmeg
Pinch of thyme
2 eggs

Soak the prunes in cold water to cover for 4 hours. Drain and put into a pan with red wine to cover and the lemon cut in thin slices. Simmer until the prunes are tender. Drain the fruit and remove the stones, and chop the prunes coarsely in the blender. Mince the pork. Cut the onion in pieces and put into the blender with the olives. Blend until finely chopped. Add to the minced pork and cook in the butter over a gentle heat until the pork is cooked but not brown. Season to taste with salt, pepper, nutmeg and thyme, cool slightly and mix with the eggs and prunes. Chill completely and use to stuff goose or duck.

Mushroom Stuffing

3oz/75g day-old brown bread
1 tablespoon parsley
1 small onion
4oz/100g mushrooms
2oz/50g butter
Salt and pepper

Break the bread into pieces and put into the blender with the parsley. Blend until the bread forms coarse crumbs. Put into a mixing bowl. Put the onion and mushrooms into the blender, and blend until finely chopped. Mix with the breadcrumbs, butter and seasoning. Use for lamb, poultry or fish. If liked, put 4oz/100g crisply cooked bacon into the blender with the onion and mushrooms.

Sage and Onion Stuffing

2 *large onions*
$\frac{1}{2}$ *pint/250ml water*
2oz/50g day-old bread
2 teaspoons fresh sage leaves
1oz/25g melted butter
Salt and pepper

Cut the onions in pieces and put into the blender with the water. Blend until the onions are coarsely chopped. Simmer for 20 minutes, and drain off the cooking liquid, but keep it in reserve. Break the bread into small pieces and blend in small quantities with the sage until the bread forms fine breadcrumbs. Mix the crumbs, sage, melted butter, seasoning, onions and enough cooking liquid to give a moist texture. Use for duck, goose or pork, or for hearts.

Sausage Stuffing

1lb/400g pork sausage meat
2oz/50g streaky bacon
Liver from poultry
1oz/25g butter
1 onion
1 egg
2oz/50g fresh white bread
2 teaspoons fresh mixed herbs
Stock
Salt and pepper

Put the sausage meat into a bowl. Cut up the bacon and liver in small pieces and fry until soft but not coloured in the butter. Put into the blender with the pan juices, the onion cut in pieces, the egg, the bread and herbs. Add enough stock to cover, and the salt and pepper. Blend until the meat is chopped in small pieces. Pour on to the sausage meat and mix thoroughly. Use for chicken or turkey.

8 Puddings, Ices and Sweet Sauces

Both the mixer and blender are useful for making sweet finishes to a meal. The blender can be used for chopping nuts, chocolate and fruit, for making breadcrumbs, and for whipping up batters and smoothing sauces. The mixer whips cream, whisks up egg whites, and makes quick pudding batters. For ice-cream making, use the blender to make the preliminary mixture smooth, and then use it again to whip up the ice once or twice during freezing. If a blender is not available, use the mixer for the same tasks. Since many families do not want to make sweet things every day, it is helpful to use the mixer and blender to produce a batch of puddings quickly at one session, and the results can then be frozen for future use.

Fruit Pancakes

½ *pint/250ml milk*
1 *large egg*
½ *teaspoon salt*
4oz/100g *plain flour*
2 *eating apples*
4oz/100g *raisins*
2oz/50g *soft brown sugar*
2 *tablespoons/30ml water*

Put the milk, egg and salt in the blender, and blend until mixed. Add the flour and blend until smooth and creamy. Fry this batter in thin pancakes. Peel and core the apples, cut in pieces, and chop finely in the blender. Simmer the apples, raisins, sugar and 2 tablespoons/30ml water until the apples are just soft. Fill the pancakes with the fruit mixture and fold over. Serve with a sprinkling of icing or caster sugar, and cream or butterscotch sauce (see page 105).

Apple Butterscotch Crumble

1½lb/600g apples
1 tablespoon/15ml water
½oz/15g butter
3oz/75g soft brown sugar
Pinch of mixed spice

Topping
3oz/75g plain flour
2oz/50g butter
1oz/25g soft brown sugar

Peel the apples and cut them in pieces. Chop coarsely in the blender and put into an ovenware dish with the water, butter, sugar and spice. Put the flour, butter and sugar for the topping into the blender, and blend until crumbly. Put on top of the apples and press down lightly. Bake at 350°F/180°C/Gas Mark 4 for 45 minutes. Serve hot with cream or custard, or with melted apricot jam.

Apple Meringue

1lb/400g cooking apples
Thin strip of lemon peel
2oz/50g sugar
1oz/25g melted butter
2 egg yolks

Meringue
2 egg whites
4oz/100g caster sugar

Use cooking apples which become fluffy when cooked. Peel and core the apples and cut them into pieces. Put into a saucepan with just enough water to cover, the lemon peel and sugar, and simmer until the fruit is soft. Cool and put into the blender with the butter and egg yolks and blend until smooth. Put into a pie dish. Whisk the egg whites until stiff with the mixer. Add half the sugar and continue whipping until stiff and glossy. Fold in the remaining sugar by hand, reserving about 1 teaspoon sugar. Spread the meringue mixture on to the apples and sprinkle on the reserved sugar. Bake at 300°F/150°C/Gas Mark 2 for 30 minutes. Serve cold. If liked, the fruit purée may be put into a baked flan case before the meringue is put on top. A mixture of fruit, such as plum and apple or blackberry and apple, may also be used.

Peach Almond Pie

8oz/200g puff pastry
1lb/400g drained canned
 peach halves
3 eggs
4oz/100g icing sugar
4oz/100g ground almonds

Line a pie plate or flan ring with the puff pastry. Arrange on it the peach halves cut side down. Put the eggs in the mixer bowl with the sugar and almonds, and whip until smooth and creamy. Pour over the peaches and bake at 400°F/200°C/Gas Mark 6 for 10 minutes, then at 375°F/190°C/Gas Mark 5 for 35 minutes. Serve with cream.

Raisin Pudding

4 × 1in/2.5cm thick slices
  bread
4oz/100g seedless raisins
¾ pint/375ml milk
Grated rind of ½ orange
2 eggs
2½oz/65g sugar
2oz/50g softened butter
Pinch of salt

Tear the bread into small pieces and blend into crumbs. Put into a bowl and mix with raisins. Put the milk, orange rind, eggs, sugar, butter and salt into the blender and blend for 20 seconds. Pour on to the crumbs and raisins, and then put the mixture into a greased pie dish. Put the dish into a roasting tin with water. Bake at 350°F/180°C/Gas Mark 4 for 1 hour. Serve hot with cream.

Bakewell Pudding

6oz/150g shortcrust pastry
2oz/50g strawberry jam
4 eggs
4 drops almond essence
4oz/100g caster sugar
3oz/75g blanched almonds
4oz/100g softened butter
1 thin strip lemon peel

Line a 7in/17.5cm pie plate with the pastry. Spread the jam on the bottom of the pastry case. Put all the other ingredients into the blender and blend for 30 seconds until well mixed. Pour into the pastry case. Bake at 425°F/220°C/Gas Mark 7 for 25 minutes.

Lemon Crumb Pudding

1in/2.5cm thick slice bread
4 eggs
2 tablespoons/30ml lemon
  juice
8oz/200g sugar
2oz/50g softened butter

Tear the bread into small pieces and blend into crumbs. Put the crumbs into a bowl. Separate the eggs. Put the egg yolks, lemon juice, sugar and butter in the blender, and blend for 20 seconds. Stir into the crumbs. Whisk the egg whites stiffly with the mixer. Fold into the crumb mixture. Put into a greased pie dish and bake at 350°F/180°C/Gas Mark 4 for 45 minutes. Serve hot with cream.

Queen of Puddings

6 × 1in/2.5cm thick slices
  bread
¾ pint/375ml milk
2oz/50g sugar
1 thin strip lemon peel
2oz/50g butter
2 eggs
1oz/25g strawberry jam
1oz/25g caster sugar

Tear the bread into small pieces and blend into crumbs. Put into a bowl. Warm the milk without boiling, and put into the blender with the sugar, lemon peel, butter and egg yolks, and blend for 10 seconds. Pour over the crumbs, stir well, and put into a greased pie dish. Bake at 325°F/170°C/Gas Mark 3 for 30 minutes. Spread the jam on top of the pudding. Whisk the egg whites with the mixer until they form soft peaks. Gradually beat in the caster sugar until the mixture is stiff and glossy. Spread on top of the jam, and continue baking for 15 minutes.

Honey Spice Pudding

2 tablespoons/30ml clear
  honey
3oz/75g butter
3oz/75g caster sugar
2 eggs
6oz/150g plain flour
1 teaspoon baking powder
½ teaspoon ground ginger
½ teaspoon ground cinnamon
Pinch of ground allspice

Sauce
¼ pint/125ml double cream
1 tablespoon/15ml clear
  honey

Grease a pudding basin and put the clear honey in the bottom. Cream the butter and sugar with the mixer on low speed. Add the eggs one at a time and then the flour sifted with the baking powder and spices. When the mixture forms a stiff dropping consistency, put into the basin, cover with foil, and steam for 1½ hours. To make the sauce, whip the cream and honey together on low speed until the mixture forms soft peaks. Serve with the hot pudding.

Apple Popovers

½oz/15g cooking fat
2 medium cooking apples
1oz/25g caster sugar
½ pint/250ml Yorkshire Pudding batter
1 lemon
1oz/25g soft brown sugar

Divide the fat between six 4in/10cm patty tins and heat at 425°F/220°C/Gas Mark 7 until the fat is very hot. Peel the apples, core and cut in slices. Toss the apples in caster sugar and divide between the tins. Make up the Yorkshire Pudding batter (see page 58) and add the grated rind of the lemon. Pour over the apples and bake for 30 minutes. Just before serving, put the juice of the lemon and the brown sugar into a saucepan, bring to the boil and boil for 2 minutes until syrupy. Serve spooned into the centres of the popovers.

Coventry Tarts

8oz/200g shortcrust pastry
8oz/200g cottage cheese
4oz/100g caster sugar
Pinch of salt
Pinch of ground nutmeg
1 tablespoon/15ml orange
  juice
2oz/50g butter
1 egg
4 tablespoons/60ml apple,
  redcurrant or cranberry jelly

Roll out the pastry to line tartlet tins. Put the cottage cheese, sugar, salt, nutmeg, orange juice, cool melted butter and egg into the blender and blend on low speed until smooth and creamy. Fill the pastry cases two-thirds full with the mixture. Bake at 375°F/190°C/Gas Mark 5 for 20 minutes until pastry is golden and the filling is set and lightly coloured. Serve freshly baked with a spoonful of jelly on each one.

Nutty Castles

2oz/50g butter
2oz/50g caster sugar
1 egg
3oz/75g self-raising flour
1oz/25g fine semolina
½ teaspoon vanilla essence
2 tablespoons/30ml milk
1oz/25g walnuts
2oz/50g mixed dried fruit

Put the butter into a mixing bowl with the sugar and cream together with the mixer on low speed. Add the egg and then the flour and semolina and increase mixer speed, gradually adding the essence and milk to make a smooth thick batter. Chop the walnuts finely in the blender and stir into the batter with the dried fruit. Put into 6 greased dariole moulds and cover with foil. Steam for 30 minutes. If tin moulds are not available, put the mixture into 6 individual ovenware dishes and bake at 375°F/190°C/Gas Mark 5 for 20 minutes. Serve hot with warm jam, or with cream or custard.

French Fritters with Cherry Sauce

4oz/100g plain flour
Pinch of salt
2 teaspoons icing sugar
8 tablespoons/120ml water
2 tablespoons/30ml oil
2 egg whites
1oz/25g caster sugar
½ teaspoon ground cinnamon
1lb/400g canned black
  cherries
½oz/15g cornflour

Put the flour, salt, icing sugar, water and oil into the blender and mix until creamy and smooth. Whisk the egg whites to stiff peaks and fold in the batter. Drop teaspoonfuls of the batter into hot oil about 1in/2.5cm deep in a frying pan and cook for about 3 minutes, turning once, until light and golden. Drain on absorbent paper and toss in a mixture of caster sugar and cinnamon. Drain the juice from the cherries and mix a little juice with the cornflour. Add to the remaining juice and bring to the boil, stirring until thick and smooth. Add the cherries and heat through, and pour over the fritters.

Fruited Fritters

4oz/100g plain flour
Pinch of salt
1 egg
6 tablespoons/90ml milk
½oz/15g icing sugar
Grated rind of 1 orange
4oz/100g mixed dried fruit
1oz/25g chopped mixed peel
2oz/50g caster sugar

Put the flour, salt, egg, milk and icing sugar into the blender and mix until smooth and creamy. Add the orange rind, dried fruit and peel. Heat about 1in/2.5cm oil in a frying pan, and fry teaspoonfuls of the mixture in the oil for about 3 minutes, turning once, until golden and crisp. Drain on absorbent paper and toss in caster sugar before serving very hot. A little warmed marmalade may be served with these fritters as a sauce.

Speedy Pudding

5oz/125g self-raising flour
1 teaspoon baking powder
4oz/100g soft butter or
  margarine
4oz/100g caster sugar
3 tablespoons/45ml milk
1 teaspoon/5ml vanilla
  essence
1 egg

Warm the heavy beater and mixer bowl with hot water while preparing the ingredients. Dry the bowl and beater, and put all the ingredients into the bowl. Starting on minimum speed, gradually increase to maximum and beat for 1 minute. Put into a greased 1 pint/500ml pudding basin, cover with foil, and steam for 1¼ hours. Try this mixture with a few spoonfuls of jam or marmalade in the bottom of the basin, or add 3oz/75g dried fruit, or the grated rind and juice of 1 lemon, or 2oz/50g cocoa. Serve with custard or a sweet sauce.

Baked Coconut Pudding

4oz/100g white bread
3oz/75g desiccated coconut
1 pint/500ml milk
1 egg
1oz/25g butter
4oz/100g sugar
Grated rind of ½ lemon
2oz/50g jam

Break the bread in pieces and make into breadcrumbs with the blender. Mix with the coconut. Bring the milk to the boil, cool slightly and put into the blender with the egg, butter, sugar and lemon rind. Blend for 10 seconds, then add the bread and coconut and blend on medium speed until well mixed. Grease an ovenware dish and spread the jam in the bottom. Put in the coconut mixture and bake at 350°F/180°C/Gas Mark 4 for 40 minutes. Serve with custard.

Sweet Soufflés

2oz/50g plain flour
½ pint/250ml milk
3 large eggs
3oz/75g butter
2oz/50g caster sugar
Flavourings

Put the flour, milk and egg yolks into the blender and blend on low speed until smooth. Melt the butter and stir in the milk mixture and sugar, cooking gently and stirring well until smooth and thick. Take off the heat. Whisk egg whites to stiff peaks with the mixer and fold into the sauce. Grease a 2 pint/1 litre soufflé dish, fill with mixture and bake at 375°F/190°C/Gas Mark 5 for 45 minutes. Serve and eat at once. This method of cooking gives a crisp crust. For a softer soufflé, stand the dish in a pan of hot but not boiling water in the oven.

Flavourings
Apple
Add 4 tablespoons sweet cooked apples and a squeeze of lemon juice to the cooked sauce, blend for 10 seconds, and fold in egg whites.

Apricot
Add 6 canned apricot halves to the cooked sauce and blend for 10 seconds before folding in egg whites.

Chocolate
Blend 2oz/50g plain chocolate with the milk mixture before cooking the sauce.

Lemon
Add the grated rind and juice of 1 lemon to the sauce before folding in the egg whites.

Liqueur
Stir in 5 tablespoons Cointreau or Grand Marnier just before folding in the egg whites.

Soft Fruit
Add ¼ pint/125ml sieved raspberries or strawberries to the cooked sauce and blend for 10 seconds before folding in the egg whites.

Baked Cheesecake

2oz/50g *digestive biscuits*
1lb/400g *cottage cheese*
1 *teaspoon lemon juice*
1 *teaspoon grated orange rind*
1 *tablespoon cornflour*
2 *eggs*
2 *tablespoons/30ml double cream*
4oz/100g *caster sugar*

Butter the sides of an 8in/20cm cake tin with removable base and line the base with greased paper. Break up the biscuits and make them into crumbs in the blender. Sprinkle the crumbs into the base of the tin. Put the cottage cheese, lemon juice, orange rind, cornflour, egg yolks and double cream into the blender and blend until smooth. Whip the egg whites with the mixer beater until they form stiff peaks. Beat in half the sugar, and then fold in the rest. Gradually fold in the cheese mixture and pour onto the base. Bake at 350°F/180°C/Gas Mark 4 for 1 hour. Turn off the oven and leave in the cheesecake until cold. Eat with fresh, frozen or canned fruit.

Cheesecakes

Refrigerated cheesecakes consist of a crunchy base and a sweet creamy topping. The blender speeds up making both parts. Try different combinations of base and topping to suit the family.

Basic Cheesecake Bases

1 Biscuit
2oz/50g *soft margarine*
1½oz/40g *caster sugar*
4oz/100g *digestive biscuits*

2 Brown Sugar
3oz/75g *soft margarine*
1oz/25g *soft brown sugar*
4oz/100g *digestive biscuits*

Melt the margarine and sugar over low heat. Break up biscuits and put into blender. Cover and blend for 10 seconds. If nuts are used, chop these in blender for 5 seconds. Stir into margarine until thoroughly combined and press into the base of a greased 8in/20cm cake tin with removable base. Leave to harden slightly before pouring in filling. For the chocolate base, melt the margarine on its own, and then add biscuits and nuts. After pressing into tin, bake at 350°F/180°C/Gas Mark 4 for 10 minutes and allow to cool before pouring on filling.

3 Walnut
2oz/50g *soft margarine*
2½oz/65g *caster sugar*
2oz/50g *walnuts*
4oz/100g *digestive biscuits*

4 Chocolate
1½oz/40g *soft margarine*
4oz/100g *chocolate digestive biscuits*
2oz/50g *walnuts*

Basic Cheesecake Filling
8oz/200g *packet full fat soft cheese*
3oz/75g *caster sugar*
2 *large eggs*
¼ *pint/125ml sour cream or yogurt (natural or fruit flavoured)*
½oz/15g *gelatine*
3fl.oz/75ml *water*

Put the pieces of cheese, sugar, egg yolks and cream or yogurt into the blender. Cover and blend for 10 seconds. Dissolve the gelatine in the water in a basin placed over a saucepan of hot water. Cool slightly and pour into the blender. Blend for 10 seconds. Whip the egg whites until stiff and gradually pour on the cheese mixture, folding it in carefully. Pour into the tin and chill until firm. Serve on metal base and garnish with cream and fruit, which may be fresh, frozen or canned. The flavour can be varied by using different fruit-flavoured yogurts (add a little orange or lemon juice and grated rind to these flavours). Sultanas or chopped mixed peel may be folded into the mixture at the last minute, or ¼ pint/125ml whipped cream may be folded in for a richer mixture.

Apple Crunch

1lb/400g *cooking apples*
Sugar to sweeten
4oz/100g *brown bread*
2oz/50g *butter*
2oz/50g *demerara sugar*
¼ *pint/125ml double cream*
2oz/50g *plain chocolate*

Peel and core the apples and cut them in slices. Put into a pan with just enough water to cover and simmer until soft. Cool and sweeten to taste. Break the bread into pieces and make into crumbs in the blender. Melt the butter in a frying pan, and add the breadcrumbs and demerara sugar mixed together. Fry gently until golden brown. Cool completely. Arrange alternate layers of apple and bread mixture in a glass serving dish, finishing with a layer of bread-crumbs. Chill in the refrigerator. Whip the cream with the mixer on medium speed, and spread on top of the crumbs. Grate the chocolate in the blender, and sprinkle over the cream.

Pineapple Nut Vacherin

3oz/75g *hazelnuts*
4 *egg whites*
7oz/175g *caster sugar*
3oz/75g *plain flour*
2oz/50g *melted butter*
1 *small fresh pineapple*
½ *pint/250ml double cream*

Put the hazelnuts into the blender and chop very finely. Whip the egg whites with the mixer until they form stiff peaks. Fold in the sugar, flour and melted butter, and the chopped nuts. Spread the mixture in four 7in/17.5cm rounds on buttered and floured cake trays. Bake at 350°F/180°C/Gas Mark 4 for 25 minutes until biscuit-coloured. Remove from trays and cool on wire racks. Peel the pineapple, cut into pieces and chop coarsely in the blender. Sprinkle with a little caster sugar. Just before serving, sandwich together layers of cake, pineapple and whipped cream. This may be served on its own, or with raspberry sauce.

Apple Batter

2lb/1kg cooking apples
Sugar to sweeten
2 tablespoons/30ml brandy
8oz/200g plain flour
½ teaspoon salt
2 eggs
1 pint/500ml milk

Peel the apples and cut them into thick slices. Cover with sugar to taste and leave to stand with the brandy poured over them. Put the flour, salt, eggs and milk into the blender and blend to a smooth batter. Grease an ovenware dish. Just before cooking, stir the apples into the batter and pour into the dish. Bake at 450°F/230°C/Gas Mark 8 for 40 minutes. Serve with a knob of butter on each serving.

Cream Crowdie

2oz/50g coarse oatmeal
1 pint/500ml double cream
2oz/50g caster sugar
1 tablespoon/15ml rum
4oz/100g raspberries or
 blackberries

Put the oatmeal into a thick pan and toss over low heat until the oatmeal is crisp. Put the cream and sugar into a mixing bowl and whip to soft peaks. Just before serving, fold in the toasted oatmeal, rum and fruit, and serve at once.

Honeycomb Mould

2 eggs
1½oz/40g caster sugar
1 pint/500ml milk
¼ teaspoon vanilla essence
½oz/15g gelatine
2 tablespoons/30ml water

Separate the eggs. Beat the egg yolks and sugar on low speed and gradually add the milk which has been heated just to the boil. Strain into a saucepan and cook over very low heat, stirring well, until the mixture coats the back of a spoon. Add the essence. Dissolve the gelatine in water and put in a basin over hot water until the gelatine is syrupy. Stir into the milk mixture and cool slightly. Whisk the egg whites to stiff peaks and fold into the milk mixture. Pour into a mould rinsed in cold water. Turn out when set and serve with cream.

Raspberry Foam

1lb/400g raspberries
3oz/75g caster sugar
½ pint/250ml double cream
2 egg whites

Put the raspberries into a bowl with the sugar and leave to stand for 1 hour to draw out the juices from the fruit. Put into the blender and blend on high speed, then sieve (or use a colander-and-sieve attachment on the mixer). Rinse out the blender and put in the raspberry purée and cream and blend on low speed until well mixed. Whisk the egg whites to stiff peaks and fold into the raspberry cream. Chill before serving with small sweet biscuits.

91

Jelly Chiffon Pie

8oz/200g shortcrust pastry
1 packet jelly
¼ pint/125ml boiling water
2 eggs
3oz/75g caster sugar
¼ pint/125ml double cream
Fruit to decorate

This is best made with a strongly flavoured jelly such as orange, raspberry or blackcurrant. Roll out the pastry and line an 8in/20cm flan ring. Prick well and line with foil and rice or beans. Bake at 425°F/220°C/Gas Mark 7 for 15 minutes. Remove foil and rice or beans and continue baking for 15 minutes until crisp and golden. Leave until cold. Put the jelly and water into a thick saucepan and heat gently until the jelly melts. Take off the heat and cool until just beginning to thicken. Put into the blender with the egg yolks and sugar and blend until smooth and creamy. Whisk the egg whites to stiff peaks and fold in the jelly mixture. Pour into the pastry case and chill. Just before serving, whip the cream and pile into the centre of the pie. Decorate with appropriate fruit. If no suitable fresh or canned fruit is available, sprinkle with chopped nuts.

Coffee Cream Flan

8oz/200g shortcrust pastry
2 tablespoons/30ml apricot
  jam
3oz/75g butter
3oz/75g caster sugar
1 egg
2oz/50g walnuts
8oz/200g self-raising flour
1 tablespoon/15ml coffee
  essence
1 tablespoon/15ml milk
¼ pint/125ml commercial
  soured cream

Roll out the pastry and line an 8in/20cm flan ring. Spread apricot jam on the base. Put the butter into the mixing bowl with caster sugar and mix on low speed until light and fluffy. Work in the egg, walnuts chopped in the blender, flour, coffee essence and milk. When the mixture is smooth and light, put into the pastry case. Bake at 425°F/220°C/Gas Mark 7 for 15 minutes, and then at 325°F/170°C/Gas Mark 3 for 30 minutes. Spread the soured cream on top and bake for 2 minutes. Serve hot.

Lilian's Lemon Flan

4oz/100g butter
8oz/200g gingernut biscuits
Juice of 2 lemons
1 small can condensed milk
¼ pint/125ml double cream

Melt the butter until just soft. Break the gingernut biscuits in pieces and make into crumbs in the blender. Mix with the butter and press into a lightly greased flan case. Put the lemon juice, condensed milk and cream in the mixer bowl, and whip to soft peaks. Pour into the flan case and chill before serving.

Refrigerator Cake

1 *tablespoon gelatine*
4 *tablespoons/60ml water*
4 *eggs*
4 *fl.oz/100ml sherry*
4 *oz/100g caster sugar*
1 *pint/500ml double cream*
1 *teaspoon vanilla essence*
24 *sponge fingers (boudoir biscuits)*
12 *almond macaroons*

Put the gelatine into the water and stand the bowl over boiling water, stirring until the gelatine has dissolved and become syrupy. Separate the eggs and put the yolks into the mixer bowl. Beat on low speed, gradually adding the sherry and the gelatine. Put into a bowl and clean the mixer bowl. Beat the egg whites to stiff peaks and add the sugar gradually, beating after each addition. Fold into the egg-yolk mixture. Whip half the cream, and fold this into the mixture, together with the vanilla essence. Line a straight-sided dish with the sponge fingers. Break up the macaroons and make them into coarse crumbs in the blender. Fill the sponge-finger mould with the cream mixture in layers, sprinkling each layer with macaroon crumbs. Chill for 12 hours in the refrigerator. Turn out and cover with the remaining cream whipped to soft peaks.

Chocolate Almond Pudding

24 *sponge fingers (boudoir biscuits)*
4 *oz/100g plain chocolate*
4 *oz/100g butter*
2 *oz/50g caster sugar*
4 *oz/100g ground almonds*
¼ *pint/125ml double cream*
2 *fl.oz/50ml milk*

Dip the sponge fingers into milk for a second so they are just moist and arrange in a neat circle in a cake tin with removable base. Melt the chocolate and pour into the mixer basin. Add the butter, sugar and almonds and beat until smooth and creamy. Whip the cream to soft peaks and fold into the chocolate mixture together with any remaining milk. Pour into the tin and leave for 12 hours in the refrigerator. Turn out and decorate with more whipped cream if liked, or some grated chocolate.

Wine Cream

3 *eggs*
1 *tablespoon/15ml redcurrant jelly*
6 *tablespoons/9ml red wine*
¼ *pint/125ml double cream*

Put the egg yolks into a basin with the redcurrant jelly and wine. Put the basin over a saucepan of hot water and stir until thick and creamy. Whip the cream to soft peaks. Whisk the egg whites to stiff peaks. Fold the cream into the slightly cooled wine mixture, and then fold in the egg whites. Put into 4 individual bowls and chill before serving.

Chocolate Chestnut Cream

5oz/125g *plain chocolate*
3oz/75g *caster sugar*
3 *tablespoons/45ml water*
1lb/400g *canned chestnut*
  purée
2 *eggs*
8oz/150g *butter*
¼ *pint/125ml double cream*

Break off 4oz/100g chocolate and put it into a bowl over hot water. Add the sugar and water and heat gently until the chocolate and sugar have melted. Put into a mixing bowl and when just cool whip in the chestnut purée, egg yolks and slightly softened butter. When the mixture is soft and creamy, whisk the egg whites to stiff peaks and fold into the chocolate mixture. Put into a lightly greased mould and chill overnight in the refrigerator. Turn out and garnish with whipped cream and the remaining chocolate grated finely.

Orange Creams

1 *packet orange jelly*
5 *tablespoons/75ml boiling*
  water
2 *egg whites*
¼ *pint/125ml double cream*

Put the jelly and water into a thick saucepan and heat gently until the jelly has melted. Put into a measuring jug and make up to ¾ pint/375ml with cold water. Stir well and leave in a cold place until just beginning to set. Whisk the egg whites to stiff peaks. Put the jelly and cream into the blender and blend until light and foamy. Fold in the egg whites and put into 4 or 6 individual dishes.

Apple Flummery

3oz/75g *pearl barley*
2 *pints/1 litre water*
1½lb/600g *eating apples*
2oz/50g *caster sugar*
Juice of 1 lemon
4 *tablespoons/60ml single*
  cream

Put the barley into the water and bring to the boil. Peel and core the apples and cut them in slices. Add to the barley and simmer until both the apples and barley are soft. Cool slightly and put into the blender. Blend until smooth and creamy. Return to the saucepan and add the sugar and lemon juice. Bring to the boil, then cool and stir in the cream. Chill before serving.

Marmalade Cream

1lb/400g *cottage cheese*
2 *tablespoons marmalade*
2 *tablespoons caster sugar*
2 *tablespoons/30ml brandy or*
  whisky
1 *tablespoon/15ml lemon*
  juice
Grated rind of 1 orange

Put all the ingredients into the blender and begin blending on low speed, scraping down if necessary. When the ingredients are well mixed, increase to high speed and blend for 10 seconds. Put into 6 individual dishes and chill for 4 hours before serving. Just before serving sprinkle with grated orange rind. This is a good pudding served with crisp shortbread.

Apricot Whip

1lb/400g can apricots in syrup
2oz/50g orange marmalade
2oz/50g blanched almonds

Put the apricots and syrup into the blender with the marmalade. Blend until smooth, and pour into a serving dish. Spread the almonds on a baking sheet and bake at 350°F/180°C/Gas Mark 4 for 5 minutes until the amonds are golden brown. If the oven is in use for any other purpose, the almonds can be browned under the grill. Scatter the almonds over the apricot whip, and chill before serving with cream.

Jelly Whip

¼ pint/125ml water
1 packet fruit jelly
1 small can evaporated milk

Boil the water in a small saucepan, reduce the heat and put in the jelly broken into pieces. Simmer until the jelly has melted. Put the evaporated milk in the blender, and blend until light and fluffy. With the blender running, pour the liquid jelly in slowly and continue blending until well mixed. Pour into a bowl and chill. If liked, blend a little fruit with the jelly, such as raspberries with raspberry jelly, or pineapple with pineapple jelly.

Lemon Flummery

½ pint/250ml water
1oz/25g butter
1 lemon
1oz/25g plain flour
4oz/200g caster sugar
1 large egg
4 digestive biscuits

Put the water into a pan with the butter and grated lemon peel, and bring to the boil. Remove from the heat and cool slightly. Put the juice of the lemon, flour and sugar into the blender, and pour on the liquid. Blend for 30 seconds. Separate the egg. Add the egg yolk and blend for 5 seconds. Put the mixture into a saucepan and bring slowly to the boil, stirring gently. Simmer for 10 minutes and pour into a bowl. Whisk the egg white with the mixer until stiff, and fold into the lemon mixture. Chill until cold and firm. Break up the digestive biscuits and blend to coarse crumbs. Sprinkle on top of the flummery, and serve with cream.

Blackcurrant Flummery

1lb/400g blackcurrants
1 pint/500ml water
½oz/15g cornflour
4oz/100g caster sugar
2 teaspoons lemon juice
2 eggs

Remove the stalks and wash the currants in cold water. Put into the water and simmer until the fruit is soft. Blend the fruit and liquid, and then sieve, or use a colander-and-sieve attachment on a mixer. Mix the cornflour with a little of the purée, then add to the remaining blackcurrant purée. Bring to the boil, add the sugar and lemon juice, and cook for 2 minutes, stirring all the time. Leave to cool, then return to the blender with the egg yolks. Blend until smooth and creamy. Whisk the egg whites to stiff peaks and fold into the blackcurrant mixture. Chill before serving with cream.

Lafayette Mousse

4 *egg whites*
12oz/300g *apricot jam or apple jelly*

If apricot jam is used, put it through a sieve or blend it until smooth before heating. Put the egg whites into a bowl and whip to soft peaks. Bring the jam or jelly to the boil and pour slowly on to the egg whites with the mixer running on low speed. Beat until the mixture is soft and even-coloured. Put into individual bowls and decorate with a few chopped nuts if liked.

Coffee Walnut Mousse

½ pint/250ml *strong black coffee*
½ pint/250ml *milk*
2oz/50g *fine semolina*
½oz/15g *gelatine*
2 tablespoons/30ml *water*
3oz/75g *caster sugar*
2 *eggs*
¼ teaspoon *vanilla essence*
2oz/50g *walnuts*
¼ pint/125ml *double cream*

Put the coffee and milk into a saucepan and heat gently. Stir in the semolina and bring to the boil, stirring well. Cook gently for 5 minutes and then remove from heat. Mix the gelatine and water and heat over a saucepan of hot water until the gelatine is syrupy. Put the coffee mixture into the blender when it is lukewarm and add the gelatine, sugar, egg yolks and essence. Blend until smooth and creamy, and pour into a bowl. Chop the walnuts finely in the blender. Whip the cream to soft peaks. Whisk the egg whites to stiff peaks. When the coffee mixture is cool, fold in the walnuts, cream and finally the egg whites. Chill before serving with small crisp biscuits.

Instant Banana Mousse

6 *bananas*
1 tablespoon/15ml *lemon juice*
2 *egg whites*
4oz/100g *caster sugar*

Cut up the bananas and put into the blender with the lemon juice. Blend until smooth and creamy. Whisk the egg whites to stiff peaks and slowly add the caster sugar, whisking until it is completely mixed with the egg whites. Pour in the banana purée and whisk until just mixed. Put into individual bowls and serve at once with cream. Honey may be substituted for half the sugar and should be blended with the bananas. A spoonful of sharp jelly such as redcurrant is very good with each portion, and should be put on each serving as a garnish.

Zabaglione

4 egg yolks
½oz/15g caster sugar
4 tablespoons/60ml Marsala
   or Madeira

A hand electric mixer may be used, so that the mixture can be heated and whisked at the same time. To use a larger mixer for the recipe, warm the bowl, add the egg yolks and sugar and whisk until thick. Pour the wine in gently and fold in by hand. Cook in a double saucepan over low heat, stirring constantly until the mixture is thick and foamy. Serve at once in warm glasses with small sweet biscuits.

Syllabub

4fl.oz/100ml white wine
1 tablespoon/15ml sherry
2 tablespoons/30ml brandy
1 lemon
2oz/50g caster sugar
½ pint/250ml double cream

Put the wine, sherry and brandy into a bowl and add the thinly grated rind and juice of the lemon. Leave to stand for 2 to 3 hours, then stir in the sugar until dissolved. Put the cream into the mixer bowl, and begin whipping on medium speed, gradually pouring in the wine mixture. Continue mixing until soft peaks form. Spoon into tall glasses and serve cold. This syllabub will hold its shape for 12 hours. The portions can be garnished with a little extra grated lemon rind.

Date Whip

8oz/200g pitted dates
4fl.oz/100ml orange juice
1 teaspoon/5ml lemon juice
4oz/100g walnut halves

Block dates are the easiest and cheapest to use for this recipe. Cut the dates into pieces and simmer the dates and orange juice together for 10 minutes. Blend for 30 seconds. Add the lemon juice and walnuts, and blend for 10 seconds until the nuts are finely chopped. Spoon into individual dishes and chill before serving. This whip may also be used to fill pastry cases, topped with whipped cream.

Fruit Mousse

12oz/300g fruit
Sugar to taste
1oz/25g powdered gelatine
1 tablespoon/15ml lemon
   juice
2 eggs

The fruit may be fresh, canned or frozen. If the fresh or frozen fruit is juicy (e.g. raspberries), no further liquid will be required. Other fruit should be cooked in a little water until just soft. Sweeten the fruit lightly to taste. Put the gelatine into 2 tablespoons/30ml water, and stand the bowl in hot water until the gelatine melts and is syrupy. Put the fruit into the blender with a little cooking liquid, or syrup from the can. Add the gelatine, lemon juice and egg yolks. Blend for 1 minute. Put into a bowl and leave in a cool place until nearly set. Whisk the egg whites with the mixer until stiff, and fold into the fruit mixture gently by hand. Leave until set.

Apple Snow

1½lb/600g cooking apples
1 teaspoon grated lemon rind
1 teaspoon/5ml lemon juice
2 tablespoons/30ml water
2oz/50g caster sugar
2 egg whites
¼ pint/125ml double cream

Use cooking apples which become fluffy when cooked. Peel and slice them, removing the cores. Put into a saucepan with the lemon rind and juice and water. Cook until the apples are soft. Put into the blender with sugar and blend until smooth. Cool. Whisk egg whites with the mixer until stiff peaks form. Turn the mixer to low speed and add the apple in small quantities until it is well mixed in. Put into a bowl. Whip the cream lightly with the mixer, and fold into the apple mixture by hand. Chill before serving. If liked, this mixture may be frozen as ice cream, beaten once during freezing.

Basic Ice Cream

¾ pint/375ml creamy milk
1 vanilla pod
2 large egg yolks
2oz/50g sugar
Pinch of salt
¼ pint/125ml double cream

Warm the milk with the vanilla pod just to boiling point. Remove the vanilla and put the milk into the blender, together with the egg yolks, sugar and salt. Cover and blend for 10 seconds. Cook the mixture in a double saucepan (or in a bowl over a pan of hot water) until the custard is of a coating consistency. Whip the cream lightly and fold into the cool custard. Pour into a freezer tray and freeze at lowest refrigerator setting for 1 hour. Scoop out the mixture into the blender, cover and blend for 10 seconds. Scrape down if necessary and continue blending until the mixture is just smooth. Return to the freezer tray and freeze for 1 hour. Repeat blending again and then freeze for 1 hour. This will give a really smooth ice cream.

Flavourings
Coffee
Scald 1oz/25g ground coffee in warm milk, and strain before blending.

Chocolate
Melt 2oz/50g plain chocolate in 4 tablespoons/60ml hot water, and add to the milk before blending.

Brown Bread Ice Cream

3oz/75g day-old brown bread
¼ pint/125ml double cream
¼ pint/125ml single cream
2oz/50g icing sugar
2 egg whites

Break the bread into pieces and make into breadcrumbs in the blender. Spread out the crumbs on a baking tray and bake at 325°F/170°C/Gas Mark 3 for 10 minutes. Whip the double cream with the mixer to soft peaks. Add the single cream and continue whipping until well mixed but not stiff. Fold in the breadcrumbs and sugar. Put into a freezer tray, and freeze for 45 minutes. Whisk the egg whites with the mixer to stiff peaks. Break up the ice cream, and whisk it with the mixer until light and soft. Fold in the egg whites. Put into the freezer tray and freeze for 2 hours.

Biscuit Tortoni

2oz/50g toasted blanched
  almonds
2 tablespoons/30ml water
2½oz/65g caster sugar
2 tablespoons/30ml sherry
3 egg yolks
8fl.oz/200ml double cream

Put the nuts into the blender and chop until coarsely ground. Take out of the blender. Put the water and sugar into a small pan, bring to the boil, and boil for 3 minutes. Put the sherry and egg yolks into the blender and blend at high speed, gradually pouring in the hot syrup. Whip the cream into soft peaks with the mixer, and then fold in the blended mixture. Put into 4 serving dishes which will resist a low temperature, and sprinkle with the ground nuts. Put into the freezing compartment of the refrigerator for 2 hours before serving.

Raspberry Water Ice

4oz/100g sugar
½ pint/250ml water
1lb/400g raspberries

The raspberries may be fresh or frozen, but frozen ones should be half-thawed before using. Put the sugar and water in a saucepan, bring to the boil, boil for 5 minutes, and then cool. Blend the raspberries and sieve them. If a colander-and-sieve attachment is available for the mixer, this may be used instead of a blender and sieve. Put the raspberry purée and sugar syrup into the blender, and blend for 15 seconds. Pour into a freezer tray and freeze for 3 hours. Half-way through freezing, blend the mixture again. For a lighter ice, fold in a stiffly whisked egg white at this stage. The same method can be used for blackberries, strawberries or blackcurrants, but blackcurrants need to be cooked in a little water before blending.

Lemon Water Ice

8oz/200g sugar
¾ pint/375ml water
2 lemons
¼ teaspoon ground ginger
Pinch of salt

Put the sugar and water into a saucepan, bring to the boil, and boil for 5 minutes. Put the thinly peeled rind of 1 lemon into the blender, with the juice of both lemons, together with the ginger and salt. Blend for 15 seconds until the rind is finely chopped. With the blender on low speed, gradually pour in the hot syrup until well blended. Pour into a freezer tray and freeze for 3 hours. During freezing time, blend the mixture once again.

Chocolate Ice Cream

2oz/50g sugar
2 tablespoons/30ml water
6oz/150g plain chocolate
3 egg yolks
½ pint/250ml double cream

Put the sugar and water into a pan, bring to the boil, and boil for 3 minutes. Break the chocolate into small pieces, and blend until the chocolate is finely chopped. With the blender running at maximum speed, pour in the hot syrup gradually and blend for 6 seconds. Add the egg yolks and blend for 5 seconds until the mixture is smooth. Whip the cream into soft peaks with the mixer, and then fold in the chocolate mixture. Put into a freezer tray and freeze for 3 hours, blending once during freezing.

Milk Ice

1 *packet fruit jelly*
$\frac{1}{4}$ *pint/125ml water*
2oz/50g sugar
2fl.oz/50ml lemon juice
1 *teaspoon grated lemon peel*
1 *pint/500ml creamy milk*

Break the jelly tablet into pieces and put into a saucepan with the water. Melt over gentle heat until syrupy. Add the sugar, lemon juice and rind and stir until the sugar has dissolved. Take off the heat and stir in the milk. The mixture may look curdled. Pour into a freezer tray and freeze for 1 hour. Put the mixture into the blender and blend until soft and creamy, or whisk with a mixer. Return to the freezer tray and freeze for 2 hours. If liked, a little appropriate fruit can be blended into the ice before the second freezing. Raspberries are particularly good with raspberry jelly, and drained canned mandarin oranges with orange or tangerine jelly. This is an inexpensive ice which children enjoy.

Fruit and Nut Ice Cream

$\frac{1}{2}$ *pint/250ml double cream*
$\frac{1}{4}$ *pint/125ml single cream*
4 *drops vanilla essence*
2oz/50g icing sugar
1 *teaspoon ground cinnamon*
2oz/50g raisins
2oz/50g sultanas
2oz/50g walnut halves
2 *egg whites*

Honey Sauce
4 *tablespoons/60ml liquid
  honey*
1 *tablespoon/15ml lemon
  juice*
1 *teaspoon arrowroot*
3 *tablespoons/45ml water*

Whisk together the double and single creams and essence with the mixer until they begin to thicken. Whisk in the sugar and cinnamon, and then fold in the raisins and sultanas. Chop the walnuts coarsely in the blender, and add to the mixture. Turn into a freezer tray, and freeze at lowest refrigerator setting for 1 hour, stirring once during freezing. Whisk the egg whites with the mixer, and fold into the ice cream. Return to the freezer tray and freeze until firm. Make the sauce by warming together the honey and lemon juice without boiling, then stirring in the arrowroot mixed with the water. Bring slowly to the boil, and cook gently until clear. Cool slightly before serving over the ice cream.

Nut Ice Cream

*6oz/150g walnut halves or
  hazelnuts*
$\frac{1}{2}$ *pint/250ml double cream*
2oz/50g sugar
1 *teaspoon/5ml vanilla
  essence*
3 *egg yolks*
$\frac{1}{2}$ *teaspoon ground ginger*

Put the nuts into the blender and chop very finely. Whip the cream lightly and fold in the nuts. Boil the sugar with 2 tablespoons/30ml water for 2 minutes. Put this syrup in the blender with essence, egg yolks and ginger and blend until smooth. Fold into the nuts and cream by hand. Put into a freezer tray, cover with foil and freeze at lowest setting for 2 hours. This ice is very good with chocolate sauce.

Raspberry Honey Ice

1lb/400g raspberries
¼ pint/125ml double cream
¼ pint/125ml natural yogurt
6fl.oz/150ml clear honey
2 tablespoons/30ml lemon
  juice
4 egg whites
Pinch of salt

Put the raspberries into the blender and blend until smooth, then sieve (or use a colander-and-sieve attachment on a mixer). Put the raspberry purée into a mixing bowl with the cream, yogurt, honey and lemon juice and mix until completely blended together. Put into freezer trays and freeze at lowest refrigerator setting for 1 hour. Whisk the egg whites and salt to stiff peaks. Put the raspberry purée into the blender and blend until just soft. Fold in the egg whites and return the mixture to freezer trays. Freeze for 2 hours before serving.

Brown Bread Cream and Fruit Sauce

¾ pint/375ml milk
3 egg yolks
1oz/25g sugar
½oz/15g gelatine
3 tablespoons/45ml water
2oz/50g brown bread
Grated rind of ½ lemon
2fl.oz/50ml double cream

Sauce
8oz/200g strawberries or
  raspberries
Caster sugar or honey

Heat the milk just to boiling point. Put the egg yolks and sugar into a mixing bowl and whip on low speed until creamy. Add the warm milk and whip together until mixed, then heat until the mixture coats the back of a spoon. Meanwhile, mix the gelatine and water and put into a basin over hot water until the gelatine is syrupy. Take the milk mixture from the heat, stir in the gelatine and leave to cool. Make breadcrumbs with the brown bread, spread them on a baking sheet and bake at 325°F/170°C/Gas Mark 3 until crisp and lightly coloured. Just before the milk mixture is completely cold, stir in the breadcrumbs and lemon rind. Whip the cream to soft peaks and fold into the mixture. Put in a cold place until serving time. Make the sauce by blending the fruit until smooth and then putting through a sieve, or use a colander-and-sieve attachment on a mixer. Sweeten to taste with caster sugar or honey. Serve the sauce in a separate bowl.

Chocolate Fudge Sauce

1oz/25g plain chocolate
½oz/15g butter
2 tablespoons/30ml milk
1 tablespoon/15ml golden
  syrup
4oz/100g soft brown sugar
½ teaspoon vanilla essence

Put the chocolate into the blender. Warm the butter, milk and syrup and pour into the blender. Blend until smooth. Return to the saucepan with the sugar and stir over low heat until the sugar has dissolved. Bring to the boil and boil steadily without stirring for 5 minutes. Take off the heat and stir in the vanilla essence. Serve hot over ice cream or steamed or baked puddings.

Whipped Sherry Sauce

2 egg yolks
1oz/25g icing sugar
4 tablespoons/60ml sweet
   sherry

This should be made with a hand electric mixer. Put all the ingredients into a basin over a pan of hot water and whisk until thick, light and foamy. Serve immediately over steamed or baked puddings, ice cream or fruit pies.

Coffee Cream Sauce

2 eggs
6 tablespoons/90ml hot strong
   coffee
2oz/50g caster sugar
Pinch of salt
¼ pint/125ml double cream

Beat the eggs on low speed and gradually beat in the coffee, sugar and salt. Put into the top of a double saucepan, or a basin over hot water, and cook without boiling until the sauce is thick enough to coat the back of a spoon. Leave until cold. Just before serving, whip the cream to soft peaks and fold into the coffee mixture. Serve over ice cream or steamed puddings.

Chocolate Sauce

4oz/100g plain chocolate
8oz/200g sugar
¼ pint/125ml hot coffee or
   milk
Pinch of salt
½ teaspoon/2.5ml vanilla
   essence

Chop the chocolate finely in the blender. Put all the ingredients into the blender and blend until smooth. Cool and store in a covered jar in the refrigerator. This sauce may be served hot or cold.

Custard Sauce

1 pint/500ml milk
1oz/25g cornflour
1 egg
1oz/25g butter
2oz/50g sugar
½ teaspoon vanilla essence

Mix a little of the milk with the cornflour. Bring the remaining milk to the boil. Pour on to the cornflour and then return to the saucepan to cook for a minute, stirring continuously. Take off the heat. Put the egg, butter, sugar and essence in the blender and blend on medium speed and pour the milk through the centre of the blender cap. Serve hot on puddings or pies, or cold with fruit.

Lemon Sauce

1 lemon
1oz/25g soft butter
½ pint/250ml water
1oz/25g cornflour
1oz/25g sugar

Cut up the lemon and remove the pips. Put into the blender with all the other ingredients and blend on high speed for 10 seconds. Strain into a pan and bring to the boil, stirring well. Continue cooking for 3 minutes. Serve hot over steamed or baked puddings.

Opposite, clockwise from the top: Baked Coconut Pudding (page 88), Raisin Pudding (page 85), Fruit Pancakes (page 83), Queen of Puddings (page 85). *Centre:* Milk Ice (page 100).

Butterscotch Sauce

8fl.oz/200ml evaporated milk
4oz/100g soft brown sugar
4oz/100g caster sugar
2oz/50g softened butter
1 tablespoon/15ml honey
½ teaspoon/2.5ml vanilla
  essence
Pinch of salt

Put all the ingredients in the blender and blend until smooth. Store in the refrigerator. This sauce may be served hot or cold.

Raspberry Sauce

8oz/200g raspberries
2oz/50g icing sugar

Blend the fruit and sugar to a thick purée, adding a little water if too thick. Put through a sieve and chill. If a colander-and-sieve attachment to the mixer is available, this may be used instead of blending and sieving.

Brandy or Rum Butter

8oz/200g unsalted butter
8oz/200g icing sugar
6 tablespoons/90ml brandy or
  rum

Cut the butter into pieces and put into the mixer bowl. Cream the butter at medium speed. Sieve the icing sugar and add gradually, beating until white and fluffy. Put in the brandy or rum drop by drop until it is well mixed. Put into a serving dish and serve with steamed puddings or mince pies.

Opposite, top left: Butterscotch Sauce (page 105) with Pancakes. *Centre:* Lilian's Lemon Flan (page 92). *Right:* Orange Jelly Whip (page 95).

9 Bread, Pastry, Cakes, Biscuits and Icings

All kinds of baked goods can be quickly made with a mixer and blender, without the hard physical labour of hand-kneading, beating or whipping. With larger mixers, it is worth doubling recipes and baking two cakes at a time, so that one can be frozen, and full advantage is taken of the time-saving qualities of a mixer.

Bread and Yeast Cakes

A dough hook is an inexpensive attachment to a mixer and saves a great deal of time and hard work. The hook may be used for the initial mixing and kneading, and for the second kneading after proving. For the best results, use 'strong' plain bread flour. Fresh yeast or dried yeast may be used, but use only half the quantity of dried yeast and allow it to froth strongly in liquid before adding to the flour. The liquid used for bread-making should be lukewarm or hand-hot. Salt is essential to good flavour, and fat improves the keeping quality.

To use the dough hook, switch on to minimum speed, increasing to Speed 1 as soon as the dough is formed, which will take about 1 minute. Add a little more flour if the dough does not leave the sides of the bowl clean, or is too soft to handle easily. If the mixture is very dry, add a little extra water (flours vary in their absorption rate). The dough should be soft but manageable, and should then be worked for another 2 minutes with the dough hook until the dough is smooth and elastic.

The dough must then be left to prove in a bowl covered with a damp cloth, or in a greased polythene bag, in a warm place. This will take 45–60 minutes in an airing cupboard or near a fire; 2 hours at average room temperature; 12 hours in a cold room or larder; 12–14 hours in a refrigerator. Cool or overnight rising is easy, and has the advantage of making a stronger dough and better bread.

After this first rising, the dough should be returned to the mixing bowl and worked again with the dough hook on minimum speed for 2 minutes. The dough can then be shaped, proved again, and then baked, according to individual recipes.

White Bread

3lb/1.5kg strong plain flour
½oz/15g salt
1oz/25g fresh yeast
1½ pints/750ml warm water
2oz/50g fat (butter,
margarine or lard)

Put flour in a large bowl, make a well in the centre, and sprinkle salt around the edge. Cream the yeast with a little warm water and pour into the well. Add remaining water and warm fat. Mix on minimum speed with dough hook for 10 seconds, then for 3 minutes until the sides of the bowl are clean and the dough is smooth and elastic. The speed of the mixer should be slightly increased during mixing. Put dough in a warm place covered with a damp cloth and leave until doubled in size. Knead again with dough hook on low speed for 3 minutes. Put into 4 × 1lb/400g greased tins, half filling them. Put in a warm place until dough reaches top of tins. Bake at 475°F/240°C/Gas Mark 9 for 15 minutes, then reduce heat to 375°F/190°C/Gas Mark 5 for 30 minutes. To test if bread is cooked, turn out of the tin and rap the bottom with the knuckles. The bread will sound hollow when cooked. Cool on a wire rack.

Wholemeal Bread

3lb/1.5kg wholemeal flour
1½ pints/750ml warm water
1½oz/40g fresh yeast
1oz/25g salt
1oz/25g sugar

Use half the flour to make a batter with all the water. Cream yeast with 2 extra tablespoons/30ml warm water and stir into the batter. Leave to stand for 15 minutes, covered with a damp cloth. Add remaining flour, salt and sugar, and mix with dough hook on lowest speed for 3 minutes. Divide dough between greased loaf tins (this amount will fit 4 × 1lb/400g loaf tins) and leave to stand in a warm place for 1 hour until dough doubles in size. Bake at 450°F/230°C/Gas Mark 8 for 45 minutes, turning loaves half way through cooking time, moving them through a right angle in the oven. Cool on a wire tray.

Basic Bun Dough

½oz/15g fresh yeast
7 tablespoons/105ml milk
1oz/25g butter
1 egg
8oz/200g strong plain flour
Pinch of salt
1oz/25g sugar

Dissolve yeast in warm milk and put into a bowl with softened butter, lightly beaten egg, flour, salt and sugar. Mix with dough hook on minimum speed for a few seconds, then increase speed slightly for 3 minutes until dough is smooth and elastic. Cover and leave to rise in warm place until double in size, about 1–1½ hours. Knead again for 3 minutes. Bake plain buns, which can be iced, or add 2oz/50g currants and sultanas to make fruit buns. Form into

107

shapes and put on greased baking tray. Leave to prove again for 15 minutes. Bake at 450°F/230°C/Gas Mark 8 for 15 minutes. Cool on a wire tray and ice with water icing. Fruit buns can be brushed with a glaze of 2oz/50g sugar dissolved in 2fl. oz/50ml milk or water while still hot.

Malt Bread

1½lb/600g *strong plain flour (or a mixture of white and wholemeal flour)*
1oz/25g *fresh yeast*
¾ *pint/750ml lukewarm water*
Pinch of salt
2 *tablespoons/30ml black treacle*
2 *tablespoons/30ml extract of malt*
2oz/50g *butter*
2oz/50g *sultanas*

Put flour into a bowl. Cream yeast with a little water. Put salt in rest of water. Add all the liquid to the flour, with treacle, malt, butter and sultanas. Knead with dough hook at low speed for 3 minutes. Put in a warm place, covered with a damp cloth, for 1 hour until double in size. Knead again for 3 minutes and put into 2 × 1lb/400g tins. Leave in warm place until the mixture reaches the top of the tins. Bake at 425°F/220°C/Gas Mark 7 for 45 minutes, turning the loaves half way through cooking time. Put on a wire tray and glaze with a syrup made from 2oz/50g sugar and 2fl. oz/50ml water. Leave to cool.

Baps

1oz/25g *yeast*
½ *pint/250ml lukewarm milk and water*
1 *teaspoon sugar*
2oz/50g *butter*
1lb/400g *plain flour*
1 *teaspoon salt*

Dissolve the yeast in the warm milk and water and pour into bowl. Add sugar, softened butter, flour and salt. Mix on minimum speed with dough hook, then increase speed slightly and knead for 3 minutes until smooth and elastic. Cover with a damp cloth, and leave in warm place for 1–1½ hours until the dough has doubled in bulk. Knead again for 3 minutes. Divide dough into 8 pieces and shape into flat ovals. Put on a greased and floured baking sheet, and leave for 15 minutes. Brush with milk and dust with flour, and press a finger into the centre of each. Bake at 425°F/220°C/Gas Mark 7 for 15–20 minutes.

Lardy Cake

8oz/200g *plain flour*
¼ *teaspoon salt*
¼ *teaspoon mixed spice*
¼oz/7g *fresh yeast*
1 *teaspoon/5g sugar*
¼ *pint/125ml warm milk*
2oz/50g *lard*
2oz/50g *sugar*
2oz/50g *dried fruit*

Put the flour, salt and spice into a warm mixing bowl. Mix the yeast and 1 teaspoon sugar together and add to the flour with the warm milk. Work with the dough hook to make a soft dough. Cover and leave in a warm place for 1 hour until double in size. Roll out on a well-floured board to ¼in/6mm thickness. Spread on half the lard, sugar and dried fruit. Fold in three, turn dough to left and roll again. Repeat with the rest of the lard, sugar and dried fruit. Roll out to an oblong 1in/2.5cm thick. Put in a deep tin and leave for 45 minutes in a warm place until well risen. Score the top in a wide diamond pattern with a knife, brush with a little sugar dissolved in water. Bake at 450°F/230°C/Gas Mark 8 for 30 minutes.

Mincemeat Pinwheel Buns

½oz/12g *fresh yeast*
2½ *fl.oz/65ml warm water*
8oz/200g *plain flour*
1 *teaspoon salt*
1oz/25g *caster sugar*
1 *egg*
Grated rind and juice of ½
  orange
4oz/100g *fruit mincemeat*
4oz/100g *prepared cooking apples*
2 *tablespoons/30ml clear honey*

Mix the yeast and warm water. Put the flour, salt, sugar, egg, orange rind and juice into a warm mixing bowl. Add the yeast liquid and work with the dough hook to make a smooth elastic dough. Put into a large lightly oiled polythene bag, loosely tied at the top, until double in size, which will take about 1 hour in a warm place. Return to the mixer and knead with the dough hook for 2 minutes. Roll out to an oblong 6 × 12in/15 × 30cm. Mix the mincemeat with the apples, which have been peeled, cored and coarsely grated. Spread this mixture on the dough, and roll up lengthwise like a Swiss roll. Cut into ½in/12mm slices and put in greased bun tins. Put the tins inside a large oiled polythene bag and leave to rise until double in size, which will take about 30 minutes in a warm place. Take out of the polythene and bake at 400°F/200°C/Gas Mark 6 for 25 minutes until golden-brown. Put on a wire rack and brush with honey while still warm.

Stollen

Batter
2oz/50g *plain flour*
½ *teaspoon sugar*
½oz/15g *fresh yeast*
4oz/100g *warm milk*

Mix the batter ingredients in a warm bowl and leave for about 30 minutes in a warm place until frothy. In a mixing bowl, cream the butter and sugar, add the egg and beat well. Add the yeast batter with all the remaining ingredients except the melted butter and icing sugar. Put on the dough hook and mix well to a soft dough. Put the bowl in a large lightly oiled polythene bag, and leave to rise until double in size, which will take about 1½ hours in a warm place. Knead the dough again with the dough hook until it is smooth and elastic. Roll out to an oval about 10 × 8in/25 × 20cm, brush with melted butter and fold over lengthwise so that the top layer is 1in/2.5cm from the edge of the bottom. Put the dough on a greased baking sheet and cover with oiled polythene. Leave to rise until

Other ingredients

2oz/50g *butter*

2oz/50g *caster sugar*

1 *egg*

6oz/150g *plain flour*

½ *teaspoon salt*

3oz/75g *raisins*

2oz/50g *quartered glacé
 cherries*

1oz/25g *mixed peel*

1oz/25g *blanched almonds*

Grated rind of ½ *lemon*

½oz/15g *melted butter*

Sifted icing sugar

½oz/15g *fresh yeast*

¼ *pint/125ml warm milk*

4 *tablespoons/60ml water*

1lb/400g *plain flour*

1 *teaspoon salt*

2oz/50g *margarine or butter*

Filling

3oz/75g *crystallized orange
 slices*

2oz/50g *crystallized
 pineapple*

1oz/25g *blanched almonds*

1oz/25g *soft brown sugar*

Pinch of ground cinnamon

Egg Wash

1 *egg*

1 *teaspoon sugar*

1 *tablespoon/15ml water*

Decoration

4oz/100g *icing sugar*

1 *tablespoon/15ml water*

1 *slice crystallized orange*

Candle and holly leaves

double in size and the dough springs back when pressed with a floured finger, which will take about 45 minutes in a warm place. Remove the polythene and bake at 375°F/190°C/Gas Mark 5 for 35 minutes until golden-brown. Cool on a wire rack. Dust with icing sugar just before serving.

Christmas Candle Ring

Prepare the yeast liquid by mixing the yeast with the warm milk and water. Put the flour and salt into a warm mixing bowl and rub in margarine or butter by hand. Add the yeast liquid and work with the dough hook until the sides of the bowl are clean and the dough is smooth and shiny. Shape into a ball and put in a large, lightly oiled polythene bag, loosely tied at the top. Leave until the dough is double in size and springs back when pressed gently with a floured finger, which will take about 1 hour in a warm place. Turn the dough on to a lightly floured board and knead until the dough is firm. Divide the dough into two and roll out both pieces to a long rectangle about 12 × 5in/30 × 12cm.

Put the orange slices, pineapple and almonds into the blender and chop coarsely. Mix with the brown sugar and cinnamon, and spread filling on both pieces of dough. Twist both pieces of dough together, shape into a circle and seal the ends. Put on a greased baking tray with a castle pudding tin or small empty can in the centre. Brush with the egg wash made by beating the egg with sugar and water. Cover with oiled polythene and leave to rise until double in size for about 45 minutes. Take off the polythene and bake at 400°F/200°C/Gas Mark 6 for 45 minutes until golden-brown. Cool on a wire rack. Mix the icing sugar and water and spoon this icing over the loaf. Cut the crystallized orange slice into six triangles and put on top of icing. Put a candle in the centre and surround with holly.

Horseshoe Tea Ring

8oz/200g *strong plain flour*
Pinch of salt
1½oz/40g *butter*
½oz/15g *fresh yeast*
1 *teaspoon caster sugar*
1 *egg*
4 *tablespoons*/60ml *warm milk*
4oz/100g *plain chocolate*
2oz/50g *flaked almonds*
2oz/50g *seedless raisins*
8oz/200g *icing sugar*

Sieve the flour with salt into a warm mixing bowl and rub in two-thirds of the butter by hand. Melt the remaining butter and leave on one side. Cream the yeast and sugar together. Put the egg and warm milk in the blender and blend until well mixed. Make a well in the centre of the flour, pour in the liquid and mix to a soft dough with the dough hook, working until the dough is smooth and shiny. Cover and leave in the bowl in a warm place until double in size, which will take about 30 minutes. Chop two-thirds of the chocolate and grate the rest and reserve. Mix the chopped chocolate, almonds and raisins together for the filling. Roll the dough into a rectangle measuring 16 × 8in/40 × 20cm, and brush with the melted butter. Sprinkle the filling over and roll up, starting with one long side. Seal the ends carefully. Lift on to a greased baking tray and form into a horseshoe shape, with the join underneath. Leave in a warm place until well risen, then bake at 425°F/220°C/Gas Mark 7 for 30 minutes until golden-brown. Cool on a wire rack. Mix the icing sugar with a little water, coat the top and sprinkle with the reserved grated chocolate.

Pastry

A mixer helps to make excellent pastry, but must be used carefully as the machine is very thorough and can quickly over-mix, which results in flat, flavourless pastry. Because the mixing process is so thorough, the proportion of fat in the pastry can be cut down, using 6oz/150g fat to 1lb/400g flour. Mixer-made pastry keeps cold during preparation, because the hands need not touch it, and this also helps to improve pastry.

The fat and flour should be rubbed in at minimum speed, increasing the speed to Speed 2 as the fat breaks up. As soon as the mixture looks like fine breadcrumbs, the water should be added or the pastry will be too short. The water should be added quickly and the mixer switched off as soon as it is incorporated. If the water is added slowly and mixed between additions, the pastry will be like rubber. A large machine is best for pastry, using the heavy beater, not the whisk.

Shortcrust Pastry

8oz/200g *fat*
1lb/400g *plain flour*
Pinch of salt
3 tablespoons/45ml *cold water*

The fat may be lard, butter, or a mixture of lard and margarine. Cut the fat into pieces and put into the mixer bowl. Switch to minimum speed and tip in the flour and salt sieved together. Gradually increase the mixer speed as the fat breaks up, until the mixture looks like fine breadcrumbs. Pour in all the water and switch off as soon as the liquid is mixed in. Roll out and use for sweet or savoury dishes.

Cheese Pastry

2oz/50g *butter*
Pinch of salt
Pinch of Cayenne pepper
6oz/150g *plain flour*
2oz/50g *cheese*
2 tablespoons/30ml *cold water*

Put the butter, salt and Cayenne pepper into the mixing bowl, switch to minimum speed, tip in flour and rub into fine crumbs, increasing the speed as the fat breaks up. Shred the cheese with a shredder attachment and add to the mixture, and then add the water. Switch off as soon as the liquid is mixed in. Roll out to use for savoury pies and flans.

Sweet Flan Pastry

4oz/100g *butter*
1 teaspoon caster sugar
Pinch of salt
6oz/150g *plain flour*
1 egg yolk
2 teaspoons/10ml cold water

Put the butter, sugar and salt into the mixer bowl, switch to minimum speed, tip in the flour and gradually increase the speed as the fat breaks up. Mix until the mixture looks like fine breadcrumbs. Stir the egg yolk and water together, add to the mixture, and switch off as soon as the liquid is mixed in. Roll out carefully as this pastry is very fragile, and use for sweet flans.

Rough Puff Pastry

6oz/150g *plain flour*
Pinch of salt
5oz/125g *butter*
3 tablespoons/45ml *iced water*

Sift the flour and salt into a mixing bowl, and add the butter cut into 1in/2.5cm pieces. Mix on minimum speed for 30 seconds. Sprinkle water over and turn off mixer as soon as the dough forms. Chill in the refrigerator for 10 minutes. Roll out on a lightly floured board into a rectangle. Fold in three, give the pastry one-half turn and roll out again. Fold and leave in the refrigerator for 15 minutes. Repeat the rolling and resting process twice more, and then roll out to use.

Potato Pastry

2oz/50g fat
4oz/100g *self-raising flour*
Pinch of salt
4oz/100g *cooked potatoes*
¼ *pint*/125ml *water*

The fat may be butter, lard or margarine. Put the fat into the mixing bowl and switch to minimum speed. Tip in the flour and salt, increasing speed as the fat breaks up. Add the potatoes which have been very well mashed, and the water and switch off as soon as all ingredients are combined. Roll out carefully; use for savoury pies.

Choux Pastry

2oz/50g *butter*
¼ *pint*/125ml *water*
4oz/100g *plain flour*
3 *eggs*

Put the butter and water into a pan and bring to boiling point. Take off the heat, add sifted flour quickly and beat over moderate heat for a few minutes until the paste forms a ball and the sides of the saucepan are clean. Cool slightly and put into the mixing bowl. Add the eggs one at a time, continuing to beat until each egg is thoroughly mixed in and the mixture is smooth and shiny. Beat on maximum speed for 30 seconds. Use for cream buns or éclairs.

Cakes, Biscuits and Icings

The use of a mixer speeds up the preparation of cakes and biscuits, but it is important not to over-beat or the results will be tough. A small hand electric mixer is useful for creaming and whisking, but it is not so suitable for rubbing in, or for heavy mixtures. Use a mixer whisk for egg whites and for light mixtures.

Some cake batters may be made in the blender, but then specially lightened, easy-creaming fats should be used, and fat should be at room temperature. When using a blender, it is usually necessary to stop the machine frequently so that the blender may be scraped down. Mixtures must not be over-blended or the cakes will be tough. The blender is a useful accessory when preparing a cake with a mixer, as it can be used for grating and chopping nuts and chocolate, or preparing breadcrumbs.

Scones

8oz/200g *self-raising flour*
Pinch of salt
2oz/50g *butter*
1oz/25g *caster sugar*
1 *egg*
2 *tablespoons*/30ml *milk*
A little milk for glazing

Sift the flour and salt into the mixing bowl. Add the butter and mix on low speed until the fat has been rubbed in. Add the sugar, egg and milk and mix to a soft dough. Turn on to a floured board and roll out lightly ¾in/18mm thick. Cut out 12 rounds and put on a baking sheet. Brush with a little milk and bake at 450°F/230°C/Gas Mark 8 for 10 minutes. Cool on a wire rack. *Cheese scones* may be made by omitting the sugar but adding 1oz/25g grated cheese. *Fruit scones* may be made by adding 2oz/50g dried fruit to the basic sweet scone mixture.

Surprise Muffins

8oz/200g self-raising flour
½ teaspoon salt
½ teaspoon mustard powder
Pepper
4oz/100g butter or margarine
2oz/50g Cheddar cheese
2oz/50g seedless raisins
1 egg
¼ pint/150ml milk

Sift the flour, salt, mustard powder and pepper into a mixing bowl. Cut the fat into small pieces and, with the mixer on low speed, work the fat into the flour, until the mixture is like breadcrumbs. Stir in the grated cheese and the raisins, and then add the egg and milk. Mix on low speed to a soft dough. Grease some deep bun tins and put in the mixture (this quantity should fill 18–20 tins). Bake at 400°F/200°C/Gas Mark 6 for 20 minutes. Split open while still warm and spread with butter, serving immediately.

Cottage Griddle Scones

1oz/25g butter
4oz/100g cottage cheese
2 eggs
2oz/50g self-raising flour
1 tablespoon/15ml milk

Melt the butter and put into a bowl with the cottage cheese. Start mixing on low speed and add the eggs one at a time. When completely mixed, add the flour and the milk to make a smooth thick batter. Drop in spoonfuls on a hot greased griddle or heavy frying pan and turn several times as the scones become set and golden. Serve freshly baked with honey, jam or jelly, or as an accompaniment to crisp hot bacon.

Walnut and Honey Scones

1lb/400g self-raising flour
1 teaspoon salt
4oz/100g butter
1oz/25g caster sugar
2oz/50g walnuts
2 tablespoons/30ml clear
  honey
¼ pint/125ml milk

Put the flour and salt into a mixing bowl and add the butter cut into small pieces. Using the mixer on low speed, work together until the mixture is like breadcrumbs. Add the caster sugar. Put the walnuts into the blender and chop coarsely. Add the walnuts, honey and milk to the flour mixture and continue beating on low speed to form a soft but not sticky dough. Turn on to a lightly floured board, and roll out to ½in/1.25cm thickness. Cut into 2in/5cm rounds with a cutter, and place close together on a greased baking sheet. Brush the tops of the scones with a little beaten egg or milk. Bake at 425°F/220°C/Gas Mark 7 for 10 minutes. These scones are very good with cheese.

Treacle Biscuits

4oz/100g lard
1 tablespoon/15ml black
  treacle
1 egg
8oz/200g plain flour
Pinch of bicarbonate of soda
4oz/100g fine oatmeal
3oz/75g granulated sugar

Melt the lard and treacle together and put into the mixing bowl. Add the egg and flour sifted with bicarbonate of soda and mix with the mixer on low speed. Gradually add the oatmeal and sugar to make a firm dough. Roll out thinly on a lightly floured board and cut into 3in/7.5cm rounds. Put on greased baking sheets, prick with a fork and bake at 350°F/180°C/Gas Mark 4 for 20 minutes. Cool on a wire rack. These are very good eaten with cheese.

Doughnuts

8oz/200g *strong plain flour*
½ *teaspoon caster sugar*
½oz/15g *fresh yeast*
6 *tablespoons/90ml warm milk*
Pinch of salt
½oz/15g *butter*
1 *egg*
1 *tablespoon/15ml red jam*
2oz/50g *caster sugar*
Pinch of ground cinnamon

Sift one-quarter of the flour into a bowl and stir in the sugar and yeast with milk. Mix with the mixer on low speed until well blended, and leave to stand for 30 minutes until frothy. Add the remaining flour, salt, butter and egg and work with the dough hook to form a light soft dough. Cover and leave to rise until double in size. Turn on to a floured board and knead lightly. Divide into 8 balls, cover and leave to rise for 30 minutes. Press a hole in each ball with a finger and put in a little jam. Pinch the edges of the dough so that the jam is covered. Deep fry in hot oil for 4 minutes until golden brown. Drain on absorbent kitchen paper and roll in caster sugar mixed with cinnamon.

Cornish Splits

1lb/400g *strong plain flour*
2oz/50g *caster sugar*
¼ *pint/125ml milk*
¼ *pint/125ml water*
1oz/25g *fresh yeast*
1 *teaspoon salt*
2oz/50g *butter*

Sieve one-quarter of the flour into a bowl and stir in 1 teaspoon sugar. Warm the milk and water together to lukewarm, stir in the yeast and add to the flour. Mix with the mixer on low speed until well blended and leave 30 minutes until frothy. Sift the remaining flour and salt and stir in the remaining sugar. Add to the yeast mixture with the melted and cooled butter and work with the dough hook to give a light soft dough. Cover and leave until double in size. Turn on to a floured board, knead lightly and divide into 14 pieces. Form into round buns and put on buttered and floured baking trays, leaving space to rise. Leave for 30 minutes. Bake at 425°F/220°C/Gas Mark 7 for 20 minutes. Cool on a wire rack, split diagonally and fill with jam and whipped cream.

Cinnamon Rolls

1lb/400g *self-raising flour*
¼ *teaspoon salt*
4oz/100g *soft margarine*
2oz/50g *caster sugar*
2 *eggs*
4fl.oz/100ml *milk*
1oz/25g *granulated sugar*
1 *teaspoon cinnamon*

Sieve the flour and salt into a mixing bowl. Cut up the margarine and add to the flour. With the mixer on low speed, work together until the mixture is like fine breadcrumbs. Stir in the sugar, eggs and milk and mix on medium speed to a firm dough. Roll out on a floured board about ½in/1.25cm thick and cut into rounds with a 3in/7.5cm cutter. Moisten the edges of each round with a little milk and fold over into half-moon shapes. Brush the tops with milk and put on a greased baking sheet. Bake at 425°F/220°C/Gas Mark 7 for 15 minutes. Brush again with milk and sprinkle with the granulated sugar and cinnamon stirred together. Return to the oven for 1 minute. Serve hot with butter.

Drop Scones

8oz/200g *plain flour*
Pinch of salt
1 *teaspoon bicarbonate of*
  soda
2 *teaspoons cream of tartar*
2oz/50g *sugar*
2 *eggs*
¼ *pint/125ml milk*
1oz/25g *softened butter*

Sift together the flour, salt, bicarbonate of soda and cream of tartar, and stir in the sugar. Put the eggs, milk and butter into the blender, and blend until smooth. Add the flour mixture and blend until thick and creamy. Cook in spoonfuls on a hot greased griddle or thick frying pan until both sides are golden. When cooked put on a wire rack and wrap in a clean cloth to keep soft. Serve spread with butter.

Apple Scones
Add 2 peeled and quartered apples to the blender with the milk mixture. Serve buttered and sprinkled with sugar and cinnamon.

Banana Scones
Put 3 thin slices of banana on each scone when cooking before turning over. Serve with butter and sugar, or with syrup.

Potato Pancakes

1lb/400g *potatoes*
1 *small onion*
2 *eggs*
2oz/50g *plain flour*
1 *teaspoon salt*
¼ *teaspoon baking powder*

Cut the potatoes into small pieces and dry them well with kitchen paper. Cut the onion in pieces. Put all the ingredients into the blender and blend until finely chopped. Stop the motor and scrape down the potatoes with a spatula if necessary. Pour this batter on to a hot greased griddle or thick frying pan and brown on each side. These pancakes are very good served hot with butter. They can also be used as an accompaniment to bacon or sausages.

Light Cakes

2 *eggs*
Juice of 1 *orange*
4oz/100g *self-raising flour*
Pinch of salt
2oz/50g *caster sugar*
4 *tablespoons/60ml sour milk*
Lard for frying
1oz/25g *soft brown sugar*

Put the eggs into the mixing bowl with half the orange juice and beat until well mixed. Sieve the flour and salt together and mix in the sugar. Add to the bowl with the milk and beat well to make a fairly thin batter. Melt a little lard in a thick frying pan and pour in spoonfuls of batter to make 2in/5cm rounds. When golden on the bottom, turn over and cook the other side. Drain on absorbent paper and serve freshly made, sprinkled with the remaining orange juice and brown sugar.

Opposite: Home-baked crusty white bread (page 107) with pickles (page 165) and beer.

10 Savoury flans can be made with a variety of fillings to serve hot or cold (pages 61–2).

13 Cheesecake with a biscuit base (page 89), garnished with fresh fruit.

Honey Biscuits

6oz/150g butter
4oz/100g sugar
2 tablespoons/30ml golden
  syrup
2 tablespoons/30ml clear
  honey
2 egg yolks
12oz/300g plain flour
Pinch of salt
½oz/15g mixed spice
½oz/15g ground ginger
½oz/15g bicarbonate of soda
1 egg white
2oz/50g mixed nuts

Put the butter and sugar into a warm bowl and cream with the mixer until light and fluffy. Heat the syrup and honey together gently, cool slightly and beat into the creamed mixture with the egg yolks. Sift together all the remaining ingredients except the egg white and nuts, and add to the creamed mixture gradually, mixing to form a firm dough. Chill in the refrigerator for 2 hours. Roll out on a floured board and cut into shapes. Put on baking sheets and brush the tops with a little lightly beaten egg white. Chop the nuts coarsely in the blender and sprinkle on the biscuits. Bake at 300°F/150°C/Gas Mark 2 for 10 minutes. Cool on a wire rack.

Victoria Sponge

4oz/100g butter or margarine
4oz/100g caster sugar
2 eggs
4oz/100g self-raising flour

Put the butter or margarine into a mixing bowl with the caster sugar, and cream on low speed until light and fluffy. Break in the eggs one at a time and continue beating. Sieve the flour and fold into the creamed mixture. Put into two greased 7in/17.5cm sponge tins. Bake at 375°F/190°C/Gas Mark 5 for 30 minutes. Leave in the tin for 2 minutes, then cool on a wire rack. Put together with jam, cream or butter icing, and ice the top if liked.

Flavourings
Chocolate
Add ½oz/15g cocoa powder with the flour.

Coffee
Add 1 teaspoon/5ml coffee essence to butter and sugar.

Lemon
Add 1 teaspoon grated lemon rind to butter and sugar.

Orange
Add 1 teaspoon grated orange rind to butter and sugar.

Vanilla
Use vanilla-flavoured sugar, or add a few drops of vanilla essence to butter and sugar.

Opposite: Scones, baps, muffins with jam, gingerbread, pastry flans, sponge cakes and fruit cakes (pages 107–29)—all these tea-time recipes can be made with a mixer or blender.

Farmhouse Sponge

4 eggs
8oz/200g caster sugar
Grated rind of ½ lemon
2oz/50g plain flour
2oz/50g cornflour

Break two eggs into a mixing bowl. Separate the remaining eggs and put the yolks in with the whole eggs. Add the sugar and lemon rind and beat on low speed until very thick. Whisk the egg whites until stiff. Sift together the flour and cornflour and fold gently into the egg-yolk mixture. Finally fold in the egg whites. Grease and line the bottom of an 8in/20cm round cake tin and grease and flour the sides. Dust the sides with a little caster sugar. Put in the sponge mixture and bake at 325°F/170°C/Gas Mark 3 for 1 hour. Cool on a wire rack and dust with a little caster sugar.

Sponge Drops

2 eggs
Pinch of salt
3oz/75g caster sugar
3oz/75g plain flour
Large pinch of baking powder
A little caster sugar
Raspberry jam
Double cream
A little icing sugar

Separate the eggs, and put the whites into a mixing bowl. Add the salt and whisk on high speed until stiff. Gradually whisk in the sugar and the egg yolks alternately until the mixture is thick and creamy. Fold in the flour sifted with baking powder and put in spoonfuls on baking sheets which have been greased and floured. Dust with a little caster sugar and bake at 450°F/230°F/Gas Mark 8 for 5 minutes. Cool on a wire rack and sandwich together with jam and whipped cream, and dust with icing sugar.

Madeira Cake

9oz/225g plain flour
1 teaspoon baking powder
Pinch of salt
6oz/150g caster sugar
6oz/150g butter
3 eggs
1 teaspoon grated lemon rind
A little milk
1 slice candied citron peel

Sift the flour with the baking powder and salt. Put the sugar and butter into a mixing bowl and beat on low speed until light and fluffy. Add the eggs one at a time, continuing to beat until very light and fluffy. Put in flour mixture and grated lemon rind and switch off mixer as soon as the flour is incorporated, adding a little milk if necessary. The mixture should shake easily from a spoon. Put into a greased and lined 7in/17.5cm cake tin and bake at 350°F/180°C/Gas Mark 4 for 1 hour 20 minutes. Put the slice of peel on the cake after 30 minutes in the oven.

Flavourings

Cherry
Omit the lemon rind and peel. Add a few drops of vanilla or almond essence to the butter and sugar, and 4oz/100g halved glacé cherries tossed in the flour.

Coconut
Omit lemon rind and peel. Add a few drops of vanilla essence to the butter and sugar. Reduce the flour to 7oz/175g, and add 3oz/75g desiccated coconut.

Farmhouse Gingerbread

8oz/200g *butter or margarine*
8oz/200g *soft brown sugar*
8oz/200g *black treacle*
12oz/300g *plain flour*
1oz/25g *ground ginger*
½oz/15g *ground cinnamon*
2 *eggs*
½ *pint/250ml milk*
½oz/15g *bicarbonate of soda*

Grease and line a tin 7 × 11in/17.5 × 27.5cm. Heat the butter or margarine, sugar and treacle until the fat has just melted. Sift the flour and spices into a bowl. Add the melted fat mixture and eggs and beat with the mixer on low speed. Warm the milk to blood heat, stir in the bicarbonate of soda, and add to the remaining mixture. Mix until just blended, but do not overbeat. Pour into tin and bake at 300°F/150°C/Gas Mark 2 for 1½ hours. This gingerbread improves with keeping, and can be served on its own, or spread with butter.

Dorset Apple Cake

8oz/200g *self-raising flour*
Pinch of salt
4oz/100g *lard*
12oz/300g *cooking apples*
4oz/100g *sugar*
2oz/50g *currants*
A little milk
3oz/75g *butter*
1oz/25g *soft brown sugar*

Sieve the flour and salt and rub in the lard with the mixer on low speed until the mixture is like breadcrumbs. Peel and core the apples and chop them coarsely in the blender. Add to the flour mixture with the sugar and currants, and enough milk to make a stiff dough. Mix well together with the mixer on low speed and put into two greased 7in/17.5cm sponge tins. Bake at 425°F/220°C/Gas Mark 7 for 10 minutes, then reduce heat to 300°F/150°C/Gas Mark 2 for 1 hour. Cool on a wire rack for 5 minutes, then sandwich together with half the butter. Cut up the remaining butter in flakes and mix with the brown sugar and sprinkle on top of the cake. Serve while still slightly warm.

Morning Cake

1 *egg*
3fl.oz/75ml *milk*
1½oz/40g *melted butter*
¼ *teaspoon/1.25ml lemon essence*
½ *teaspoon/2.5ml vanilla essence*
4oz/100g *caster sugar*
5oz/125g *plain flour*
1 *teaspoon baking powder*
Pinch of salt

Put egg, milk, melted butter and essences into the blender. Blend until smooth. Add sugar and blend for 5 seconds. Sift the flour, baking powder and salt, and add to the blender. Cover and blend for 10 seconds. Pour into a greased rectangular tin (about 10 × 7in/25 × 17.5cm) and bake at 350°F/180°C/Gas Mark 4 for 25 minutes. Cut into squares and serve warm. For a variation, cover the surface of the batter closely with stoned fresh plums or cooked prunes, or a thick layer of thinly sliced apples. Sprinkle with 2oz/50g sugar and a pinch of cinnamon before baking. This can be served as a cake, or with cream or custard.

Applesauce Cake

12oz/300g *cooking apples*
4oz/100g *butter*
8oz/200g *sugar*
8oz/200g *plain flour*
Pinch of ground cloves
1 *teaspoon ground cinnamon*
1 *teaspoon bicarbonate of*
soda
4oz/100g *seedless raisins*
2oz/50g *nut kernels*

Peel, core and cut up the apples, and just cover with water. Simmer until soft and then blend until smooth. Cream the butter and sugar with the mixer on low speed until light and fluffy. Measure ½ pint/250ml apple purée and add to the creamed mixture, together with the flour sifted with spices and bicarbonate of soda. Chop the raisins and nuts in the blender and fold into the cake mixture. Put into a 7in/17.5cm greased round cake tin and bake at 350°F/180°C/Gas Mark 4 for 1 hour.

Banana Nut Loaf

2oz/50g *walnut halves*
8oz/200g *plain flour*
1 *teaspoon salt*
1 *teaspoon bicarbonate of*
soda
3 *small bananas*
2 *eggs*
6oz/150g *sugar*

Put the walnuts into the blender and blend until finely chopped. Put into a bowl with the flour, salt and soda. Cut the bananas into small pieces, put into the blender and blend until mashed. Stop the motor and scrape down the banana with a spatula. Add the eggs and sugar and blend until well mixed. Pour on to dry ingredients in bowl and mix well. Put into a small greased loaf tin and bake at 350°F/180°C/Gas Mark 4 for 1 hour. Cool on a rack before slicing and spreading with butter or cream cheese. This is also good toasted.

Bran Fruit Loaf

4oz/100g *All-Bran cereal*
5oz/125g *caster sugar*
10oz/250g *mixed dried fruit*
½ *pint/250ml milk*
4oz/100g *self-raising flour*

Put the cereal, sugar and dried fruit into a mixing bowl and stir them well together. Add the milk and mix on minimum speed until well mixed. Leave to stand for 30 minutes, then mix in the flour. Pour into a well-greased 2lb/1kg loaf tin. Bake at 350°F/180°C/Gas Mark 4 for 1 hour. Turn out of the tin and cool on a wire rack. Cut in slices and eat spread with butter.

Walnut Loaf

12oz/300g *plain flour*
2 *teaspoons baking powder*
Pinch of salt
8oz/200g *sugar*
2 *eggs*
½ *pint/250ml milk*
1½oz/40g *melted butter*
4oz/100g *walnut halves*

Sift together the flour, baking powder and salt. Put the sugar, eggs, milk and butter into the blender and blend at high speed until well mixed. Add the walnut halves and blend on low speed until they are finely chopped. Pour on to the flour mixture, and mix on low speed. Put into a greased 2lb/1kg loaf tin and leave to stand for 20 minutes. Bake at 350°F/180°C/Gas Mark 4 for 1¼ hours. Cool, slice and spread with butter and honey.

Chocolate Bran Cake

2oz/50g All-Bran cereal
¼ pint/125ml milk
4oz/100g butter
4oz/100g soft brown sugar
2 eggs
4oz/100g self-raising flour
3oz/75g plain chocolate
4oz/100g raspberry,
   strawberry or apricot jam

Icing
4oz/100g plain chocolate
1oz/25g butter

Put the cereal and milk into a basin and leave until the milk has been absorbed. Cream the butter and sugar with the mixer until light and fluffy. Add the eggs one by one, with a little flour. Add the milk and cereal mixture and the remaining flour, and the chocolate melted over hot water. Put into two greased 7in/17.5cm sponge tins. Bake at 350°F/180°C/Gas Mark 4 for 35 minutes. Cool on a wire rack. Put the cakes together with the jam. For the icing, melt the chocolate with the butter over hot water, and pour over the surface of the cake.

Chocolate Brownies

8oz/200g granulated sugar
1½oz/40g cocoa powder
3oz/75g self-raising flour
Pinch of salt
2 eggs
2 tablespoons/30ml creamy
   milk
4oz/100g melted butter or
   margarine
2oz/50g nut kernels
4oz/100g plain chocolate
1oz/25g butter

Stir together the sugar, cocoa powder, flour and salt in the mixer bowl. Add the eggs, milk and melted fat, and mix on low speed until well mixed, but do not overbeat. Chop the nuts in the blender and add to the mixture. Pour into a rectangular tin about 8 × 12in/ 20 × 30cm and bake at 350°F/180°C/Gas Mark 4 for 30 minutes. Cool in the tin and then pour on the chocolate melted with the butter. Cool until the chocolate has set and cut into squares.

Brown Sugar Brownies

6oz/150g soft brown sugar
3oz/75g melted butter
1 egg
5oz/125g self-raising flour
Pinch of salt
Few drops of vanilla essence
2oz/50g walnut halves

Put the sugar and butter into the mixer bowl and beat on low speed until creamy. Add the egg, flour, salt and essence and beat until just mixed. Chop the walnuts in the blender and add to the mixture. Grease a Swiss Roll tin and put in the mixture. Bake at 350°F/180°C/Gas Mark 4 for 25 minutes. Cool in the tin and cut into squares.

Chocolate Crumb Cake

8oz/200g *sweet biscuits*
4oz/100g *butter*
1oz/25g *sugar*
1oz/25g *cocoa*
1 *tablespoon*/15ml *golden
  syrup*
4oz/100g *plain chocolate*

Break up the biscuits and blend a few at a time to make fine crumbs. Melt the butter with the sugar, cocoa and syrup until just liquid. Mix in the biscuit crumbs and press into a greased tin about 1in/2.5cm deep. Melt the chocolate over hot water and pour on top of the cake. Chill for 5 hours before cutting in squares to serve.

Chocolate Meringues

2 *egg whites*
Pinch of salt
Pinch of cream of tartar
6oz/150g *caster sugar*
6oz/150g *chocolate chips* or
  plain chocolate

Beat the egg whites, salt and cream of tartar with the mixer whisk on low speed until soft peaks form. Add the sugar slowly, beating all the time until stiff peaks form. Fold in the chocolate chips, or plain chocolate chopped roughly in the blender. Cover baking sheets with Bakewell paper or plain paper (e.g. typing paper) and drop on the mixture by rounded teaspoonsful. Bake at 300°F/150°C/Gas Mark 2 for 25 minutes. Turn the meringues over carefully and continue baking for 15 minutes until crisp. Cool slightly and remove from paper, then cool on a wire rack. Store in a tin, and do not fill with cream.

Chocolate Macaroons

2 *egg whites*
4oz/100g *caster sugar*
4oz/100g *ground almonds*
1½oz/40g *drinking chocolate
  powder*
Rice paper
Blanched almonds

Whisk the egg whites with the mixer until stiff peaks form. On low speed, fold in the sugar, ground almonds and drinking chocolate powder. When just mixed, switch off the mixer. Line baking sheets with rice paper, and spoon on the mixture in small heaps. Put a blanched almond in the centre of each one. Bake at 350°F/ 180°C/Gas Mark 4 for 20 minutes. Cool on a wire rack.

Chocolate Truffle Cakes

4oz/100g *stale cake*
4fl.oz/100ml *double cream*
½oz/15g *cocoa powder*
2oz/50g *chocolate vermicelli*

Break the cake into pieces and make into very fine crumbs in the blender. Mix together the cream, cocoa and cake crumbs with a mixer so that a smooth paste is formed. Leave in the refrigerator for 1 hour. Shape into 12 balls and roll in chocolate vermicelli. Keep in a cool place until serving time. The truffles may be flavoured with a little rum or brandy if liked.

Apricot and Almond Gateau

7oz/175g butter
2oz/50g caster sugar
4oz/100g sweet biscuits
4oz/100g day-old bread
5oz/125g plain flour
2½oz/65g ground almonds
½ pint/250ml double cream
1 small can apricot halves
A little icing sugar

Cream the butter and sugar together with the mixer until light and fluffy. Make the biscuits into crumbs in the blender. Make the bread into crumbs in the blender and spread out the crumbs on a baking sheet. Put into the oven set at 325°F/170°C/Gas Mark 3 for 5 minutes. Cool the crumbs, then put the biscuit crumbs, breadcrumbs, flour and almonds into the creamed mixture and mix until well blended. Divide the mixture in two pieces and press each piece into an 8in/20cm flan ring on baking trays. Bake at 325°F/170°C/Gas Mark 3 for 20 minutes. Cool on a wire rack. Whip the cream lightly and divide in half. Drain the apricots and chop them coarsely in the blender. Fold them into half the cream and sandwich together the cakes with the mixture. Sprinkle the top of the cake with a little icing sugar, and pipe on the remaining whipped cream in a decorative pattern.

Coffee Cake

4oz/100g self-raising flour
Pinch of salt
2oz/50g butter
4oz/100g caster sugar
3 eggs

Icing
4oz/100g butter
2 teaspoons/10ml coffee
  essence
6oz/150g icing sugar
3oz/75g chopped browned
  almonds

Sift together the flour and salt. Melt the butter gently until soft, but do not brown. Put the sugar and eggs into the mixing bowl, and whisk until pale and thick. Add the melted butter, flour and salt, and mix on low speed until just mixed. Put into a lined 6in/15cm square tin and bake at 350°F/180°C/Gas Mark 4 for 40 minutes. Cool on a rack. To make the icing, put the butter, essence and sugar into the mixing bowl and whisk until soft and creamy. Cut the cake in half, spread on a thin layer of icing and put the two halves together. Spread remaining icing on top of cake and sprinkle with almonds.

Golden Pineapple Cake

3 eggs
3oz/75g dark soft brown
  sugar
3oz/75g plain flour
1 small can pineapple rings
½ pint/250ml double cream
¼ teaspoon/2.5ml vanilla
  essence
1oz/25g dark brown sugar

Put the eggs and sugar into the mixing bowl and whisk together until thick and creamy. Fold in the flour lightly and put into two greased 7in/17.5cm sponge tins lined with greaseproof paper. Bake at 350°F/180°C/Gas Mark 4 for 35 minutes. Turn out and cool on a wire rack. Drain the pineapple rings and chop them coarsely in the blender. Whip the cream and reserve half of it. Mix the remaining half with the chopped pineapple, essence and brown sugar. Put this mixture between the two cakes. Cover the top cake with the remaining cream. If liked, decorate with a few chopped nuts.

Chocolate Nut Gateau

4 *eggs*
9oz/225g *caster sugar*
6oz/150g *plain flour*
1oz/25g *cocoa powder*
2 *teaspoons baking powder*
5 *tablespoons/75ml milk*
2oz/50g *butter*

Filling
1lb/400g *icing sugar*
1oz/25g *drinking chocolate*
  powder
4oz/100g *butter*
4 *tablespoons/60ml milk*
3oz/75g *walnut kernels*
2oz/50g *chocolate vermicelli*

Put the eggs into the mixing bowl and beat lightly. Add the sugar slowly and beat until the mixture is thick and creamy. Sieve the flour, cocoa and baking powder twice. Fold the sieved mixture into the creamed fat. Heat the milk and butter gently together until the butter has just melted and fold into the cake mixture. Put into two greased and floured 8in/20cm sponge tins and bake at 375°F/190°C/Gas Mark 5 for 35 minutes. Turn out and cool on a wire rack, then split each cake in half. To make the filling, sieve the sugar and drinking chocolate powder together. Melt the butter, take off the heat and add the milk. Beat gradually into the sugar with the mixer until the icing is soft and smooth. Chop the nuts finely in the blender. Spread one-quarter of the icing on to one round of cake. Sprinkle on one-third of the nuts. Repeat the layers, and then decorate the top and sides with the remaining icing. Sprinkle with chocolate vermicelli.

Icebox Cake

4oz/100g *butter*
6oz/150g *icing sugar*
2 *eggs*
Flavourings
48 *sponge finger biscuits*
½ *pint/250ml double cream*

Cream the butter and sugar with the mixer until light and fluffy and work in the eggs one at a time. Add the flavourings and beat until fluffy. Put 12 biscuits on a flat dish, curved side down. Put on one-third of the creamed mixture. Top with another layer of the biscuits laid in the opposite direction. Cover with more creamed mixture. Continue with layers, ending with biscuits. Cover with foil and chill for 3 hours in the refrigerator. Cover completely with whipped cream and serve.

Flavourings

Lemon
Add 2 teaspoons grated lemon rind and 2 tablespoons/30ml lemon juice.

Chocolate
Add 4oz/100g melted plain chocolate and a few chopped hazelnuts if liked.

Coffee
Add 2 teaspoons/10ml coffee essence. If liked, add a few chopped walnuts and/or a few drops of rum.

Orange Rock Cakes

3oz/75g butter
3oz/75g caster sugar
1 egg
1 orange
8oz/200g plain flour
2 teaspoons baking powder
1oz/25g chopped mixed peel

Cream the butter and sugar until light and fluffy. Add the egg and the grated rind and juice of the orange together with the flour sifted with baking powder. When mixed to a soft dough, stir in the peel. Place in small heaps on greased baking tins and bake at 400°F/200°C/Gas Mark 6 for 15 minutes. Cool on a wire rack.

Chocolate Almond Biscuit Cake

4oz/100g butter
4oz/100g drinking chocolate
 powder
4oz/100g caster sugar
2 tablespoons/30ml water
4oz/100g ground almonds
1 egg
4oz/100g Petit Beurre
 biscuits
¼ pint/125ml double cream
1oz/25g blanched almonds

Put the butter into the mixing bowl with the drinking chocolate and cream together with the mixer on low speed. Mix the sugar and water and heat gently until the sugar melts. Add the ground almonds to the butter mixture and, with the mixer on low speed, work in the sugar and the egg. When the mixture is smooth and creamy, break the biscuits into small pieces and stir into the chocolate. Put into a greased 7in/17.5cm square tin and leave to set in the refrigerator. Decorate with whipped cream and almonds.

Chocolate Orange Cake

4oz/100g soft margarine
4oz/100g caster sugar
2 eggs
4oz/100g self-raising flour
Grated rind of 1 orange

Icing
2oz/50g plain chocolate
3 tablespoons/45ml water
1oz/25g soft margarine
6oz/150g icing sugar

Cut up the margarine and put into the mixing bowl with sugar, eggs, sieved flour and orange rind. Beat on low speed until ingredients are blended, and then on higher speed until the cake mixture is soft and light. Put into a greased 8in/20cm tin with the bottom lined with greaseproof paper. Bake at 350°F/180°C/Gas Mark 4 for 35 minutes. Cool on a wire rack.

Make the icing by putting the chocolate, water and margarine into a bowl over a saucepan of boiling water and stirring until the chocolate melts and the mixture is thick. Remove the bowl from the heat, cool slightly and beat in the icing sugar until the icing is of coating consistency. Pour over the cake and leave to set.

Butter Icing (Mixer)

4oz/100g *butter*
6oz/150g *icing sugar*
Flavourings

Warm the bowl and mixer beater. Put butter, sugar and flavouring into the bowl and mix on low speed until light and fluffy.

Butter Icing (Blender)

2 *tablespoons*/30ml *liquid*
4oz/100g *butter*
6oz/150g *icing sugar*
Flavourings

The liquid may be fruit juice, thin cream or strong coffee. The butter should be soft but not melted. Put all the ingredients into the blender and blend until smooth and light.

Flavourings
Chocolate
Add ½oz/15g cocoa or 2oz/50g melted plain chocolate.

Coffee
Add 2 teaspoons/10ml coffee essence.

Lemon
Add 1 teaspoon/5ml lemon juice and 1 teaspoon grated lemon rind (or a few drops of lemon essence).

Mocha
Add ½oz/15g cocoa and a few drops of coffee essence.

Orange
Add 2 teaspoons/10ml orange juice and 1 teaspoon grated orange rind (or a few drops of orange essence).

Vanilla
Add a few drops of vanilla essence.

Glacé Icing

8oz/200g *icing sugar*
2 *tablespoons*/30ml *hot water*
Flavourings

Sieve the icing sugar into the mixing bowl. Switch on to minimum speed and add water slowly until the desired consistency is reached. Use the same flavourings as for Butter Icing.

Mocha Fudge Icing

6oz/150g *plain chocolate*
1½oz/40g *soft butter*
1 *egg*
1 *teaspoon/5ml vanilla essence*
3oz/75g *icing sugar*
¼ *pint/125ml hot strong coffee*

Cut the chocolate in pieces and chop finely in the blender. Put all the ingredients into the blender except the coffee. Blend for 5 seconds. Remove cover and pour in hot coffee. Blend for 15 seconds. This gives a very creamy texture, but more icing sugar can be added slowly to give a firmer icing if preferred. This gives enough icing to fill and top a 7in/17.5cm cake.

Cream Cheese Icing

2fl.oz/50ml *double cream*
½ *teaspoon/2.5ml vanilla or lemon essence*
6oz/150g *cream cheese*
1oz/25g *soft butter*
14oz/350g *icing sugar*

Cut the cream cheese into small pieces. Put the cream, essence, cream cheese and butter into the blender. Cover and blend for 15 seconds. Add one-third of the sugar and cover. Blend for 30 seconds. While the motor is running, add the remaining sugar through the hole in the lid, and blend until smooth. This gives enough icing to fill and top a 7in/17.5cm cake.

American Frosting

1lb/400g *granulated sugar*
¼ *pint/125ml water*
Pinch of cream of tartar
2 *egg whites*
1 *teaspoon/5ml vanilla essence*

Dissolve the sugar in the water over low heat. Add the cream of tartar, and boil until the syrup forms a soft ball when dropped into cold water. Whisk the egg whites on maximum speed until stiff but not dry. Pour the hot syrup on to the egg whites with the mixer running and whisk until the frosting stands in stiff peaks, which will take about 5 minutes. Add the essence during the last seconds of mixing. This frosting sets very quickly and should be put on the cake as soon as prepared.

Flavourings
Caramel
Substitute soft brown sugar for granulated.

Chocolate
Add 3oz/75g melted plain chocolate during the last seconds of mixing.

Orange
Use 3 tablespoons/75ml orange juice in place of some of the water. Add a pinch of grated orange rind and a little orange food colouring.

Royal Icing

1lb/400g icing sugar
2 egg whites
1 tablespoon/15ml lemon
 juice
1 tablespoon/15ml glycerine

Sieve the icing sugar. Put the egg whites, lemon juice and glycerine into the mixing bowl and switch on minimum speed, using the heavy beater. Tip in a little sugar at a time, beating until smooth. Continue adding sugar until the mixture is dull-looking and very white, and forms peaks.

Confectioner's Custard

2oz/50g sugar
2 egg yolks
Few drops of vanilla essence
½ pint/250ml milk
1oz/25g plain flour
½oz/15g butter

Put the sugar, egg yolks, essence, milk and flour into the blender and blend for 30 seconds until creamy. Put into a thick pan and cook gently, stirring well, until thick. Add butter and cool. Use for filling cakes, choux pastry, slices, and the bases of the fruit flans.

Opposite, clockwise from top right: Chocolate Banana Milk Shake (page 148), Meal-in-a-glass (page 147), Eggnog (page 155), Fresh Fruit Shake for Slimmers (page 148), Iced Chocolate (page 150). *Centre:* Banana Flip (page 148).

10 Spreads, Pastes and Dips

The mincer and blender may be used to transform small quantities of meat, poultry, fish or cheese into economical spreads for sandwiches, toast or cocktail canapés. Only process small quantities of these foods at a time in a blender, as they can be thick and tend to slow up the blending process. Cheese in particular needs frequent scraping down with a spatula, with the blender motor switched off. Full fat soft cheese is easier to blend and particularly suitable for making creamy party dips. Flavoured butters may also be made in the blender to use as spreads or to serve as a dressing with vegetables, fish or meat. If yogurt is used in a recipe, add it slowly and blend as little as possible, because blending thins the yogurt. All kinds of spreads and dips should be refrigerated after blending and before use, and will become a little firmer when chilled.

Meat Paste

6oz/150g cooked meat
2oz/50g cooked bacon
1 teaspoon/5ml French mustard
1 teaspoon/5ml Worcestershire sauce
2oz/50g butter
Pepper
Garlic salt

Cut the meat and bacon into pieces. Put into the blender with mustard, sauce, softened butter and seasonings, and blend until creamy.

Opposite: A selection of drinks, dips and soups made with the blender.

Chicken Spread

4 tablespoons/60ml
  mayonnaise
1oz/25g chutney
1 stick celery
1 small onion
½ teaspoon salt
½ teaspoon/2.5ml vinegar
6oz/150g cooked chicken
2 hard-boiled eggs

Put the mayonnaise and chutney into the blender. Put the celery and onion in the blender with the salt and vinegar. Blend until the celery and onion are coarsely chopped. Cut the chicken and eggs into pieces. Add to the blender and continue blending until all the ingredients are finely chopped. Use as a sandwich filling.

Chicken Liver Herb Spread

1 tablespoon/15ml salad oil
1 medium onion
8oz/200g chicken livers
Sprig of parsley
Sprig of thyme
1 garlic clove
Salt and pepper

Put the oil into a small pan. Cut the onion into pieces and cook it for a few minutes in the oil until it is just transparent. Remove from oil and put into a blender. Put the chicken livers into the oil with chopped herbs and garlic clove, and cook until the liver is just done. Be careful not to overcook the liver, or the texture and flavour will be spoiled. Cool for 5 minutes, then add liver and herbs to the blender and blend until smooth, seasoning to taste.

Corned Beef Spread

7oz/175g corned beef
8fl.oz/200ml milk
½oz/15g plain flour
Pepper
1oz/25g butter

Cut the corned beef into cubes and put into the blender with milk, flour and a shake of pepper. Blend until smooth. Melt the butter over low heat and pour on the corned-beef mixture. Cook gently over low heat until the mixture thickens and comes to the boil. Simmer for 2 minutes. Chill before using. This is good as a sandwich filling, or as a spread for toast which can be topped by a few crisp raw onion rings.

Devilled Ham

4oz/100g cooked ham
3 hard-boiled eggs
1 small onion
1oz/25g chutney
1 tablespoon/15ml
  mayonnaise
½ teaspoon curry powder

Cut the ham, eggs and onion into pieces. Put into the blender and add the chutney, mayonnaise and curry powder. Blend to required smoothness. The mixture may be creamy, but a slightly rough texture is often more attractive, particularly if spread on toast.

Liver and Bacon Spread

6oz/150g *pig's liver*
2 *rashers streaky bacon*
1 *medium onion*
1 *garlic clove*
2oz/50g *butter*
Salt and pepper

Cut the liver and bacon into small pieces, and slice the onion and garlic. Fry the bacon, onion and garlic in half the butter. Fry the liver in remaining butter. Put the blender on low speed, and gradually put in the ingredients, blending until smooth, and seasoning to taste.

Anchovy Spread

12 *anchovy fillets*
2 *tablespoons/30ml*
 mayonnaise
3 *tablespoons/45ml double*
 cream
1 *slice onion*
¼ *teaspoon mustard powder*
6oz/150g *full fat soft cheese*

Drain the anchovy fillets to get rid of oil in can. Rinse the fillets in a little water and pat dry with kitchen paper. Put into the blender with the mayonnaise, cream, onion and mustard powder. Cover and blend for 10 seconds. Cut up the cheese into small cubes. With the motor running, drop cheese through opening in lid, and continue blending until smooth. It may be necessary to stop the motor once or twice and push down the mixture with a spatula to ensure smooth blending. Use this spread on cocktail biscuits or squares of toast, or as a filling for small sandwiches.

Kipper Spread

2 *kippers*
1 *teaspoon/5ml prepared*
 mustard
2oz/50g *butter*
Pepper
1 *tablespoon/15ml vinegar*

Cook the kippers in boiling water until tender. Take out large bones, and put the flesh into the blender with the other ingredients. Blend for 30 seconds. Use on toast or on cocktail canapés.

Salmon Spread

1 *small onion*
1 *stick celery*
4 *tablespoons/60ml*
 mayonnaise
1 *sprig parsley*
2 *tablespoons/30ml lemon*
 juice
8oz/200g *can salmon*
2 *hard-boiled eggs*
Salt and pepper

Cut the onion and celery into pieces and put into the blender with the mayonnaise, parsley and lemon juice. Blend until the vegetables are finely chopped. Drain the salmon and add the flesh to the blender with the coarsely chopped eggs, salt and pepper. Blend until the eggs are finely chopped. As canned salmon is often rather salty, do not add much salt to the blender, and adjust seasoning if necessary after blending.

Sardine Spread

2 tablespoons/30ml
  mayonnaise
1 teaspoon/5ml made
  mustard
2 tablespoons/30ml lemon
  juice
1 thin slice onion
3½oz/90g can sardines
1 hard-boiled egg
Salt and pepper

Put the mayonnaise, mustard, lemon juice and onion into the blender, and blend until the onion is finely chopped. Drain the sardines, and chop the egg roughly. Put into the blender with the onion mixture and blend until just mixed. Season with salt and pepper to taste.

Seafood Spread

8oz/200g shrimps, prawns or
  crabmeat
2 sticks celery
½ green pepper
¼ pint/125ml mayonnaise
1 thin slice onion
2 tablespoons/30ml lemon
  juice
1 tablespoon/15ml
  horseradish sauce
Pinch of salt
Few drops of Tabasco sauce

Cut the shrimps or prawns in pieces or break up the crabmeat. Cut the celery and green pepper in pieces. Put all the ingredients into the blender. Cover and blend for 30 seconds. It may be necessary to stop the motor once or twice and push down the mixture with a spatula to ensure smooth blending. Use this spread as a dip with potato crisps or small cocktail biscuits. It is also good served as a sauce with baked jacket potatoes.

Caraway Cheese Spread

2 tablespoons/30ml beer
1 teaspoon caraway seeds
4oz/100g Cheddar cheese

Put the beer and caraway seeds into the blender. Cut the cheese into small pieces and put them through the lid of the blender with the motor running. Blend until well mixed. Leave to stand for 30 minutes before using, so that the caraway seeds soften slightly.

Cheese and Bacon Spread

3 tablespoons/45ml salad
  cream
1oz/25g chutney
8 stuffed olives
4oz/100g Cheddar cheese
4 rashers cooked bacon

Put the salad cream, chutney and olives in the blender. Cut the cheese in small pieces and add to the blender. Blend until olives and cheese are coarsely chopped. Add crumbled crisp bacon, cover and blend for 15 seconds. Use on biscuits or in sandwiches.

Cheese and Tomato Spread

8oz/200g *full fat soft cheese*
1 *medium tomato*
1 *thin slice onion*
Pinch of salt
Pinch of paprika

Cut the cheese in small pieces and put into the blender. Dip the tomato in boiling water and remove the skin. Cut in pieces and take out the pips. Put the tomato flesh into the blender with the onion, salt and paprika. Blend until smooth. This is very good on cocktail biscuits.

Cheese Rarebit Spread

1 *tablespoon/15ml beer*
1 *small onion*
4oz/100g *Cheddar cheese*

Put the beer into the blender with the onion cut in quarters. Blend until the onion is finely chopped. Cut the cheese into small chunks and put through the lid of the blender with the motor running. Blend until well mixed. This can be used in sandwiches, or spread on toast.

Quick Cheese and Bacon Toasts

8oz/200g *Cheddar cheese*
8 *rashers lean bacon*
1 *medium onion*
1 *teaspoon dry mustard*
Thick slices of bread

Cut the cheese into pieces. Grill the bacon until crisp and break into pieces. Peel the onion and cut into pieces. Put the cheese, bacon and onion into the grinder, and chop very finely. Mix with the mustard. Toast the bread slices on one side only. Spread the cheese mixture on the other side and grill under medium heat until the cheese is golden and bubbling.

Flavoured Butters

Flavoured butters are useful as spreads for bread or pancakes, as a base for sandwiches, and as dressings for meat and fish. The butter should be at room temperature, and blended at low speed until smooth, stopping the machine to scrape down if necessary. Additions such as nuts or herbs should be made only when the butter is well creamed, and the blender should then be run on high speed just until the additions are coarsely chopped.

Honey Butter
Add 4 tablespoons/60ml liquid honey and a pinch of salt to 4oz/100g butter. Use for toast or biscuits.

Maple Butter
Add 4 tablespoons/60ml maple syrup, 2 tablespoons/30ml liquid honey and 2oz/50g walnuts to 4oz/100g butter. Use for pancakes or waffles.

Honey Orange Butter

Add 4 tablespoons/60ml liquid honey, a pinch of salt and the grated rind of ½ orange to 4oz/100g butter. Use for toast or biscuits.

Garlic Butter

Add 1 garlic clove and a pinch of salt to 4oz/100g butter. Use for rolls, French bread, or grilled meat.

Parsley Butter

Add 6 sprigs parsley and a squeeze of lemon juice to 4oz/100g butter. Use for grilled meat or fish, or to spread bread for sandwiches.

Watercress Butter

Add ½ bunch washed and dried watercress, pinch of salt, 1 tablespoon/15ml lemon juice and a pinch of celery seed to 4oz/100g butter. Use for grilled meat or fish.

Peanut Butter

8oz/200g salted peanuts
3 tablespoons/45ml salad oil

Put the peanuts into the blender. Cover and blend until the nuts are chopped finely. Add the oil and continue blending until smooth. For crunchy peanut butter, remove about one-third of the nuts before adding the oil. Blend the mixture to the required consistency and then stir in the remaining chopped nuts. For a slightly sweet peanut butter, add a little honey during the blending. If you like a really fresh-tasting butter, buy peanuts in the shell, roast them in the oven and shell them. Measure out the same amount of peanuts and blend them with their brown skins on and a little salt.

Avocado Dip

1 lemon
1 large ripe avocado
4 tablespoons/60ml salad oil
2 garlic cloves
1 small onion
Salt and pepper

Peel the lemon and remove the pips. Cut in pieces and blend until very finely chopped. Cut the avocado in half and spoon the flesh into the blender. Add the oil, garlic and coarsely chopped onion in the blender with the salt and pepper. Blend until smooth, and chill. This is very good served with pieces of cucumber and celery, and with crisps.

Aubergine Dip

2 *medium aubergines*
2 *lemons*
4*fl.oz*/100*ml salad oil*
½ *teaspoon salt*
2 *large garlic cloves*

Trim the aubergines and split them in half lengthwise. Put them cut side down on an ungreased baking sheet and bake at 400°F/ 200°C/Gas Mark 6 for 45 minutes until the skins are crisp. Cool and scrape the flesh from the skins. Remove the pips from the lemons and cut the flesh and peel into small pieces. Blend the lemons until very finely chopped. Add the aubergine flesh and blend until smooth. Add the oil, salt and garlic cloves, and blend until smooth again. Serve chilled with sticks of raw vegetables.

Basic Soft Cheese Dip

6*oz*/150*g full fat soft cheese*
Salt and pepper
A little milk
Flavourings

Cut the cheese into small pieces and put into the blender with salt and pepper and a little milk, and blend to a dipping consistency. Add flavouring ingredients and blend until they are finely chopped and mixed with the cheese. Serve chilled with potato crisps, pieces of celery, cucumber or raw carrot, or small cocktail biscuits.

Flavourings
Curry Dip
Add 2 teaspoons/10ml Worcestershire sauce, ¼ teaspoon curry powder, and 2oz/50g pineapple if liked.

Crunchy Dip
Add 2oz/50g celery, 2oz/50g apple and 2oz/50g walnuts.

Anchovy Dip
Add 2oz/50g drained anchovy fillets and ½ teaspoon/2.5ml lemon juice.

Fish Dip
Add 7oz/175g drained canned tuna or salmon and 1 teaspoon/5ml Worcestershire sauce.

Blue Cheese Dip

1 *medium carrot*
1 *small onion*
3 *tablespoons/45ml commercial sour cream*
3 *sprigs parsley*
1 *garlic clove*
Salt and pepper
4 *drops Tabasco sauce*
8oz/200g *cottage cheese*
4oz/100g *Danish Blue cheese*

Cut the carrot and onion into pieces. Put all the ingredients except the cottage cheese and blue cheese into the blender, and blend until the vegetables are finely chopped. Add the cottage cheese and blend until well mixed. It will be best to start at low speed, then change to high speed to work in the cheese. Cut the blue cheese in small pieces and add to the blender. Blend until smooth and chill before using. Serve with crisps or raw vegetable sticks.

Hot Cheddar Dip

8oz/200g *Cheddar cheese*
1 *pint/500ml milk*
2oz/50g *plain flour*
½ *teaspoon curry powder*
2oz/50g *butter*
1 *dessertspoon/10ml tomato purée*
Salt and pepper

Cut the cheese into small pieces and put gradually into the blender with the motor running, so that it is grated. Transfer to a bowl. Put the milk, flour and curry powder into the blender, and blend until well mixed. Melt the butter and pour in the milk mixture. Cook over a moderate heat, stirring well, until the mixture boils. Simmer for 3 minutes, then stir in the cheese and continue heating gently until the cheese melts. Stir in the tomato purée, with salt and pepper to taste. Serve hot with crisps or cubes of bread. The dip can be kept hot for a time over a small hot-plate.

Cocktail Dip

4 *rashers lean bacon*
½oz *grated horseradish*
¼ *pint/250ml commercial sour cream*
4 *tablespoons/60ml mayonnaise*
1 *slice onion*
½oz/15g *fresh parsley*

Grill the bacon until crisp and then crumble into small pieces. Put all the ingredients into the blender. Cover and blend for 30 seconds until the mixture is smooth. Put into a serving bowl and chill for 1 hour. Serve with potato crisps, small cocktail biscuits or sticks of fresh vegetables such as celery, carrots and cucumber. This dip can also be used for a quick sauce on baked jacket potatoes, roast beef or grilled steak.

Devilled Egg Dip

2 tablespoons/30ml vinegar
2 tablespoons/30ml mustard
 pickle
2 tablespoons/30ml
 mayonnaise
2fl.oz/50ml commercial sour
 cream
1 small onion
Salt and pepper
4 drops Tabasco sauce
2 sprigs parsley
6 hard-boiled eggs

Put all the ingredients except eggs into the blender, and blend until smooth. Cut the eggs in quarters and add to the blender. Blend until the eggs are finely chopped. Chill before using. This is good with crisps, carrot sticks or small cocktail sausages.

Horseradish Dip

4 tablespoons/60ml commercial sour cream
1 small onion
¼ teaspoon salt
1oz/25g grated horseradish
2 drops Worcestershire sauce
8oz/200g full fat soft cheese

Put the sour cream, coarsely chopped onion, salt, horseradish and Worcestershire sauce into the blender. Blend until the onion is finely chopped. Cut the cream cheese into small pieces and add to the blender slowly. Blend until smooth and chill before using. This is good served with small hot cocktail sausages.

Pickle Dip

3 tablespoons/45ml
 mayonnaise
2 tablespoons/30ml single
 cream
4oz/100g salted peanuts
1 sprig parsley
6 pearl cocktail onions
1 tablespoon/15ml tomato
 ketchup
1 tablespoon/15ml sweet
 pickle

Put all the ingredients in the blender, and blend until the nuts are finely chopped. Serve with crisps and cocktail sausages to dip.

Salad Dip

1 *small cucumber*
1 *small green pepper*
3 *spring onions*
1 *garlic clove*
½ *teaspoon fennel seeds*
Pinch of thyme
Salt and pepper
4*fl.oz/100ml natural yogurt*

Remove ends from the cucumber, and cut it in chunks without peeling. Remove the seeds from the green pepper and cut into pieces. Trim the spring onions, keeping some of the green tops. Put cucumber, pepper, onions and garlic into the blender, and blend until the vegetables are finely chopped. Add the fennel, thyme, salt, pepper and yogurt, and blend for 5 seconds until yogurt is mixed in. Chill before using with crisps or small cocktail biscuits.

Seafood Dip

8*oz/200g crabmeat*
4*oz/100g shrimps*
8*oz/200g full fat soft cheese*
¼ *pint/125ml natural yogurt*
1 *tablespoon/15ml tomato sauce*
1 *tablespoon/15ml lemon juice*
Salt and pepper

Put the crabmeat and shrimps into the blender and chop finely. Add the remaining ingredients and blend until smooth. Serve with crisps or small biscuits. The crabmeat and the shrimps may be fresh, canned or frozen.

Tomato Yogurt Dip

4*oz/100g tomatoes*
1 *teaspoon basil*
1 *garlic clove*
Salt and pepper
4 *fl.oz/100ml natural yogurt*

Dip the tomatoes into boiling water and remove the skins. Cut in pieces, take out the pips, and drain off the juice. Put into the blender and blend until smooth. Add the basil and garlic and blend until the garlic is finely chopped. Put in salt and pepper and the yogurt and blend for only 5 seconds until the dip is smooth. As a variation, use marjoram and cottage cheese, instead of basil and yogurt.

11 Drinks

With a blender in the kitchen, it is possible to produce a huge range of delicious drinks quickly, easily and economically. For a quick and nourishing drink for children, hot chocolate can be made in the usual way, then whirled in the blender to give a foamy, creamy topping. An easy milk shake need consist of no more than well-chilled milk and a scoop of ice cream blended until creamy and frothy. Health-food addicts will find a blender invaluable for mixing their own special drinks of raw fruit or vegetables, yogurt and wheat germ, or eggs and milk. A juice separator attachment to a mixer makes it even easier to produce healthy drinks, with such mixtures as citrus fruit juice and herbs, or a mixture of fruit and vegetable juices.

To speed up the processing of drinks, it is a good idea to make up a simple sugar syrup which can be stored in the refrigerator. This can be used for many kinds of sweet drinks, milk shakes, and alcoholic drinks. Crushed ice is another essential for many drinks, and many types of blender can be used for crushing cubes. It is important, however, to check the manufacturer's instructions for your individual model before using it for ice-crushing. If the machine is not suitable for crushing ice alone, break up ice cubes into five or six pieces with a hammer wrapped in cloth, and put the ice pieces into the liquid which is being blended. Start blending drinks on low speed, gradually increasing to high speed. Try to control timing carefully, as drinks are spoiled by over-blending. If soda water or other carbonated drinks are to be added, put these into drinks after blending.

All kinds of drinks are made doubly attractive by suitable garnishing. A sprinkling of ground nutmeg or cinnamon looks good on milk drinks, or a grating of chocolate or sprinkling of instant coffee on appropriate iced drinks. A whirl of whipped cream is tempting on hot milk drinks as well as on milk shakes. A stick of cinnamon

145

makes a stirrer for both milk drinks and fruit punches. Fresh herbs such as borage and mint look cool on chilled fruit or alcoholic drinks, and so do thin slices of orange, lemon, unpeeled apple or cucumber.

Basic Sugar Syrup

8oz/200g granulated sugar
½ pint/250ml warm water

Put the sugar and water into the blender, and blend until the sugar has dissolved. Store in a covered container in the refrigerator. This sugar syrup is the best sweetener for both alcoholic drinks and for fruit and milk drinks, as it leaves no sugar residue and makes a smooth drink.

Chocolate Syrup

6oz/150g plain chocolate
1 pint/500ml boiling water
1lb/400g granulated sugar
½ teaspoon/2.5ml vanilla
  essence

Break the chocolate into small pieces and put into the blender with the water, sugar and essence. Blend until the sugar has dissolved and the syrup is smooth. Store in a covered container in the refrigerator. This is excellent for milk shakes and ice-cream sodas, and can also be added to plain hot or cold milk for a quick drink.

Tomato Cocktail

1lb/400g ripe tomatoes
6 ice cubes
½ teaspoon salt
Pepper
2 teaspoons/10ml lemon juice
1 teaspoon sugar

Dip the tomatoes into boiling water and remove the skins. Cut in pieces and discard the pips. Wrap the ice cubes in a cloth and break with a hammer or rolling pin. Put all the ingredients into the blender and blend for 30 seconds. Serve at once. If preferred, a few drops of Worcestershire sauce may be substituted for the lemon juice. *This is enough for 4 servings.*

Tomato Juice

1lb/400g fresh tomatoes
¼ pint/125ml water
1 small onion
1 teaspoon/5ml lemon juice
1 teaspoon/5ml wine vinegar
½ bay leaf
Pinch of celery salt
1 teaspoon sugar

Put all the ingredients into a saucepan and simmer for 10 minutes. Remove the bay leaf and put the remaining ingredients into the blender. Cover and blend for 10 seconds. Strain into a jug and leave in a cold place for 2 hours. Stir well before serving and pour into small glasses. *This is enough for 6 servings.*

Carrot and Pineapple Cocktail

½ pint/250ml pineapple juice
1 thin slice lemon
1 large carrot
Pinch of salt

Chill the juice before using. The lemon slice should retain the peel, but not pips. Cut the carrot into pieces. Put all the ingredients into the blender and blend for 1 minute. Serve chilled. *This is enough for 2 servings.*

Vegetable Health Drink

6 sprigs watercress
2 sprigs parsley
1 stick celery
4 tomatoes
4in/10cm cucumber
1 small onion
1 teaspoon/5ml lemon juice
Salt and pepper
½ pint/250ml water

Cut the watercress, parsley and celery in pieces. Skin the tomatoes and cut them in pieces, and cut the cucumber in pieces. Peel the onion and cut it in pieces. Put all the vegetables into the blender with the lemon juice, seasonings and water, and blend until smooth. Serve very cold. *This is enough for 2 servings.*

Meal-in-a-glass

1 standard egg
½ pint/250ml orange juice
1 tablespoon/15ml liquid
  honey
1 tablespoon/15ml lemon
  juice
½oz/15g wheat germ

Put all the ingredients into the blender, and blend for 30 seconds. *This is enough for 1 serving.*

Yogurt Shake

¼ pint/125ml yogurt
1 thin slice lemon
½oz/15g caster sugar
¼ pint/125ml pineapple juice

Put all the ingredients into the blender and blend for 30 seconds. If buttermilk is available, this can be used instead of yogurt. Some fresh fruit, such as pineapple or banana can also be added. *This is enough for 2 servings.*

Ice-Cream Soda

2 ice cubes
2oz/50g raspberries or
  strawberries
½oz/15g sugar
2oz/50g vanilla ice cream
¼ pint/125ml soda water

Wrap the ice in a tea towel and break each cube into four or five pieces with a hammer or rolling pin. Put the fruit, sugar, crushed ice cubes and ice cream into the blender, and blend until smooth. Strain into a tall glass and add soda water. *This is enough for 1 serving.*

Milk Shake

¼ pint/125ml chilled milk
1oz/25g ice cream
Sugar and flavouring

Put all the ingredients in the blender. Cover and blend for 10 seconds. Pour into a long glass. Milk shakes can be flavoured with commercial milk-shake syrup, drinking-chocolate powder, instant coffee, and soft fruit. Vanilla ice cream can be used, or a flavoured ice cream to blend with the other flavourings. *This is enough for 1 serving.*

Chocolate Banana Milk Shake

½ pint/250ml milk
1 ripe banana
½oz/15g drinking chocolate
  powder
2oz/50g vanilla ice cream

Cut the banana into quarters. Put all the ingredients into the blender. Cover and blend for 15 seconds. Pour into a tall glass and serve at once. *This is enough for 1 serving.*

Fresh Fruit Shake for Slimmers

6oz/150g fruit
4 ice cubes
1pint/500ml slimmers' milk
Artificial sweetener to taste

The best fruits to use are strawberries, raspberries, peaches, apricots or bananas. Fruit may be fresh, canned or frozen. Canned fruit should be well drained before use, and frozen fruit should be just thawed. Wrap ice cubes in a cloth and break with a hammer or rolling pin. Put all the ingredients into the blender and blend for 1 minute until smooth. *This is enough for 3 servings.*

Banana Flip

2 bananas
½ pint/250ml milk
4oz/100g cottage cheese
½oz/15g soft brown sugar

Cut the bananas into pieces and put into the blender with the milk. Blend for 30 seconds. Add the cottage cheese and sugar and blend again for 15 seconds. Serve cold. *This is enough for 2 servings.*

Malted Milk Shake

1 pint/500ml milk
3oz/75g Horlicks powder
2 teaspoons lemon juice
½ pint/250ml soda water
4oz/100g vanilla ice cream

Put the milk, Horlicks powder and lemon juice into the blender and blend until smooth and creamy. Pour into glasses, top up with soda water and add a spoonful of ice cream to each glass. Serve at once with straws. *This is enough for 4 servings.*

Nursery Shake

2 medium bananas
4 tablespoons/60ml rosehip
 syrup
1½ pints/750ml chilled milk
2oz/50g vanilla ice cream
Pinch of grated nutmeg

Cut the bananas in pieces. Put into the blender with the syrup, milk and ice cream and blend until smooth and creamy. Pour into glasses and dust lightly with nutmeg. *This is enough for 4 servings.*

Tropical Shake

2 medium bananas
1 orange
4 tablespoons/60ml pineapple
 juice
1 pint/500ml chilled milk
2oz/50g vanilla ice cream

Cut the bananas in pieces. Grate the rind from the oranges and reserve. Squeeze out the juice and put into the blender with the bananas, pineapple juice, milk and ice cream. Blend until smooth and creamy, pour into glasses and sprinkle on the grated orange rind. *This is enough for 4 servings.*

Almond Flip

1 egg white
1oz/25g ground almonds
1oz/25g icing sugar
½ teaspoon almond essence
1 pint/500ml milk
Pinch of ground cinnamon

Whisk the egg white to stiff peaks and fold in the almonds, sugar and essence. Warm the milk just to the boil and add to the mixing bowl, folding into the egg white at low speed. Pour into mugs and sprinkle with cinnamon. *This is enough for 3 servings.*

Chocolate Cream Whip

1½oz/40g drinking chocolate
 powder
3 tablespoons/45ml boiling
 water
1½ pints/750ml chilled milk
2fl.oz/50ml double cream
2oz/50g milk chocolate

Mix the chocolate powder and boiling water to a paste. Put into the blender with the milk and blend until smooth. Pour into glasses and top with whipped cream and grated chocolate. *This is enough for 4 servings.*

Iced Chocolate

1oz/25g drinking chocolate
  powder
2fl.oz/50ml hot coffee
¾ pint/375ml cold milk
4oz/100g chocolate ice cream
Whipped cream
1oz/25g grated chocolate

Mix the drinking chocolate powder and the hot coffee. Put into the blender with milk and ice cream and blend until smooth. Pour into tall glasses and top with whipped cream and grated chocolate. *This is enough for 2 servings.*

Iced Coffee

4 ice cubes
½ pint/250ml strong black
  coffee
1oz/25g sugar
¼ pint/125ml single cream
Sweetened whipped cream
  (optional)
2fl.oz/50ml brandy
  (optional)

Wrap the ice cubes in a cloth and break with a hammer or rolling pin. Put the coffee, ice and sugar into the blender, and blend for 30 seconds. Add the cream and blend on low speed until well mixed. Pour into glasses and top with whipped cream if liked. If brandy is used, blend with the coffee in the goblet. *This is enough for 2 servings.*

Mexican Chocolate

2oz/50g plain chocolate
½oz/15g instant coffee powder
4 drops vanilla essence
Pinch of ground cinnamon
¾ pint/375ml hot milk

Cut the chocolate into squares and put into the blender with the coffee powder, essence, cinnamon and milk. Blend until chocolate has dissolved and serve at once. *This is enough for 2 servings.*

Strawberry Melon Cooler

1 ripe honeydew melon
1 teaspoon fresh mint leaves
½ pint/250ml water
6oz/150g strawberries
1oz/25g honey

Cut the melon in half and scoop out the seeds. Scoop out the flesh and put into the blender. Blend for 30 seconds. Add the mint leaves, water, strawberries and honey, and blend for 30 seconds until smooth. Serve chilled. *This is enough for 4 servings.*

Four Fruit Flip

¾ pint/375ml pineapple juice
1 banana
1oz/25g nuts
½oz/15g raisins
1 small eating apple

Put the pineapple juice in the blender. Cut the banana into pieces, and add to the blender with the nuts and raisins. Do not peel the apple, but cut into pieces and remove the core. Add to the blender, and blend for 45 seconds until smooth. Serve chilled. *This is enough for 4 servings.*

150

Hawaiian Punch

2 slices fresh or canned
  pineapple
1 medium orange
1 banana
¾ pint/375ml water
Ice cubes

Cut the pineapple into chunks. Peel the orange, remove pips, and cut flesh into quarters. Cut the banana into pieces. Put all the ingredients into the blender, cover and blend for 30 seconds. Put ice cubes or crushed ice into glasses, and pour over the punch. *This is enough for 4 servings.*

Peach Ginger

2 large ripe peaches
3oz/75g caster sugar
¼ teaspoon ground ginger
Pinch of nutmeg
2 tablespoons/30ml lemon
  juice
½ pint/250ml ginger beer
1 small orange

Dip the peaches in boiling water to loosen the skins. Peel the peaches and cut them into small pieces. Put into the blender with the sugar, ginger, nutmeg and lemon juice. Blend for 30 seconds. With the motor running, pour in ginger beer and then switch off blender at once. Pour into glasses and garnish with the orange cut in thin slices. *This is enough for 3 servings.*

Mint Cooler

Large bunch of mint leaves
¼ pint/125ml Basic Sugar
  Syrup
Juice of 3 lemons
¼ pint/125ml lime juice
1¾ pints/1 litre iced water

Strip the leaves from their stems, but reserve four small sprigs for garnish. Put the leaves into the blender with the warm syrup and blend until the mint is well chopped. Leave to stand for 5 minutes, and then strain. Mix the lemon and lime juice and put into the blender with the mint liquid. Blend for 2 seconds and pour into a jug with the iced water. Stir and garnish with fresh mint. *This is enough for 6 servings.*

Honey Lemonade

4 lemons
3oz/75g honey

Peel the lemons and remove the pips. Cut the flesh into pieces and blend for 30 seconds. Add the honey and blend until the honey is incorporated. Store in the refrigerator, and dilute with water to serve. About 3 tablespoons/45ml of concentrate to ½ pint/250ml water will be the right proportion.

Orange and Lemon Cup

1 *orange*
1 *lemon*
1 *pint/500ml water*
1oz/25g *sugar*
4 *ice cubes*

Do not peel the orange and lemon. Cut them into pieces and remove pips. Put into the blender with water and sugar. Wrap the ice cubes in a cloth and break with a hammer or rolling pin. Add the ice to the blender. Blend for 2 minutes. Strain and serve at once. *This is enough for 2 servings.*

Lemon Cordial

1 *thin-skinned lemon*
2oz/50g *sugar*
6 *ice cubes, crushed*
1¼ *pints/625ml water*

Do not peel the lemon, but cut it into pieces. Put into the blender with the other ingredients. Cover and blend for 10 seconds. Strain and pour into tall glasses, and garnish with a few fresh mint leaves. *This is enough for 3 servings.*

Lemon Squash

2 *large lemons*
4 *pints/2 litres water*
3lb/1.5kg *sugar*
2oz/50g *citric acid*

Peel the lemons thinly, avoiding the white pith. Put the peel into the blender with ½ pint/250ml water, and blend for 1 minute. Put into a saucepan with the remaining water and bring to the boil. Extract juice from the lemons (using a juice extractor attachment if available). Add the juice, sugar and acid to the saucepan. Stir well to dissolve the sugar and bring to the boil. Strain and pour into hot sterilized bottles. Store in a cold place for up to two weeks. To serve, dilute with water or soda water.

Orangeade

2 *thin-skinned oranges*
1½ *pints/750ml water*
12oz/300g *sugar*
1 *teaspoon citric acid*
Orange food colouring

Cut the oranges in pieces without peeling and remove the pips. Put into the blender with a little of the water and chop finely. Dissolve the sugar in remaining water and bring to the boil for 5 minutes. Cool and put into the blender with the oranges, citric acid and a little food colouring. Blend until smooth. Cool, strain and bottle, and store in the refrigerator. Dilute with water or soda water to taste.

Basic Daiquiri

6 *ice cubes*
3fl.oz/75ml *light rum*
1fl.oz/25ml *lime juice*
½oz/15g *sugar*

Wrap the ice cubes in a cloth and break with a hammer or rolling pin. Put all the ingredients into the blender and blend on low speed for 15 seconds. If liked, a little canned, frozen or fresh fruit may be added to the blender, such as peaches or strawberries. *This is enough for 1 serving.*

Moscow Mule

2fl.oz/50ml vodka
1 teaspoon lime juice
¼ pint/125ml ginger beer
2 ice cubes
Sprig of fresh mint

Put the vodka and lime juice into the blender. Blend on low speed for 30 seconds and pour into a glass with the ginger beer. Add ice cubes and a sprig of mint to garnish. *This is enough for 1 serving.*

Winter Evergreen

2 ice cubes
2fl.oz/50ml Pernod
1fl.oz/25ml dry vermouth
1 egg white
1 teaspoon icing sugar

Put the ice cubes in a cloth and break them into smaller pieces with a hammer. Put into the blender with the Pernod, vermouth, egg white and icing sugar. Blend on low speed for 30 seconds and pour into a glass. *This is enough for 1 serving.*

Hot Foaming Coffee

2 eggs
1oz/25g caster sugar
2 tablespoons/30ml Tia
   Maria coffee liqueur
½ pint/250ml strong black
   coffee
½ pint/250ml milk
Pinch of grated nutmeg

Put the egg yolks and sugar into the blender with the coffee liqueur, and blend on low speed until just mixed. Heat the coffee and milk together and pour into the blender. Blend until well mixed and pour on to stiffly whisked egg whites. Pour into mugs and sprinkle with nutmeg. *This is enough for 4 servings.*

Winter Milk Punch

2 pints/1 litre milk
1oz/25g ground almonds
4oz/100g caster sugar
1 teaspoon grated orange rind
1 teaspoon grated lemon rind
4 tablespoons/60ml rum
6 tablespoons/90ml brandy
2 egg whites

Put the milk into a thick saucepan with the almonds, sugar and grated rinds. Bring just to the boil and take off the heat. Stir in the rum and brandy. Whisk the egg whites to stiff peaks and fold in the milk mixture. Pour into mugs and serve at once. *This is enough for 8 servings.*

Basic Sour

4 ice cubes
1½ fl.oz/40ml lime or lemon
    juice
½oz/15g sugar
3 fl.oz/75ml whisky, rum or
    brandy

Wrap the ice cubes in a cloth and break with a hammer or rolling pin. Put all the ingredients into the blender and blend on low speed for 15 seconds. Serve garnished with orange slices and maraschino cherries. *This is enough for 1 serving.*

Whisky Cooler

2 ice cubes
2 fl.oz/50ml whisky
4 fresh mint leaves
½oz/15g sugar
2 teaspoons/10ml lemon juice

Wrap the ice cubes in a cloth, and break with a hammer or rolling pin. Put all the ingredients into the blender and blend on low speed for 30 seconds. Strain into a glass, top up with soda water, and garnish with sprigs of fresh mint and lemon slices. *This is enough for 1 serving.*

Gin Fizz

4 ice cubes
2 fl.oz/50ml gin
1 tablespoon/15ml lemon
    juice
1 thin strip lemon rind
½oz/15g sugar
1 egg white

Wrap the ice cubes in a cloth, and break with a hammer or rolling pin. Put all the ingredients into the blender, and blend on low speed for 30 seconds. Pour into a glass, top up with soda water, and garnish with lemon slices. *This is enough for 1 serving.*

Rum and Pineapple Shake

4 ice cubes
2 fl.oz/50ml light rum
2 slices fresh pineapple
½oz/15g sugar

Wrap the ice cubes in a cloth, and break with a hammer or rolling pin. Put all the ingredients in the blender, and blend on low speed for 1 minute. *This is enough for 1 serving.*

Honey Eggnog

1 tablespoon/15ml clear
    honey
2 eggs
1 pint/500ml milk

Put the honey, eggs and milk into the blender and blend on low speed until smooth and creamy. The milk may be either cold or hot and the drink is very nourishing for children or invalids. *This is enough for 2 servings.*

Bloody Mary

3 ice cubes, crushed
½ pint/250ml tomato juice
¼ pint/125ml vodka
2fl.oz/50ml lime juice
Pinch of salt
Pinch of celery salt
½ teaspoon/2.5ml
   Worcestershire sauce
Few drops of Tabasco sauce

Be sure the ice cubes are well broken up before putting into the blender. Put in all the ingredients, cover and blend for 15 seconds. *This is enough for 4 servings.*

Eggnog

3 standard eggs
½ pint/250ml milk
2oz/50g sugar
¼ pint/125ml brandy, rum,
   whisky or sherry
½ pint/250ml single cream
3 ice cubes, crushed

Put all the ingredients into the blender. Cover and blend for 10 seconds. A warm drink may be made by leaving out the ice, and warming the milk and cream. Add them slowly through the opening in the lid until the mixture is creamy, and sprinkle nutmeg on each serving. *This is enough for 4 servings.*

12 Preserves and Pickles

The blender and the mincer attachments of a mixer are invaluable aids to making jam, mincemeats, marmalades and a variety of pickles and sauces. With these mechanical aids, both fruit and vegetables can be chopped coarsely or finely, or minced quickly. Not only will time be saved in the chopping process, but also the cooking time will be shortened, particularly in the case of marmalade.

Fruit and vegetables may be minced without liquid, while powerful grinders and choppers can process dry ingredients. When a blender is used, the process will be speeded up and the machine will not be strained if some liquid from the recipe is included with the bulky ingredients.

Always use a large heavy pan for making jams and pickles, so that it remains stable on a stove, will not burn easily, and will not allow the mixture to boil over. A little butter rubbed round the jam pan will prevent the formation of scum which otherwise needs to be removed and may be wasted. Jam and marmalade should be cooked just to setting point, when the mixture flakes off a wooden spoon, or wrinkles on a cold plate. Chutney needs to be cooked much longer until the surplus liquid has evaporated and the mixture is thick and brown.

Jars for all kinds of preserves and pickles must be completely clean and heated in a very low oven until used, so that hot mixture can be poured into them without damage. Jams should be covered with a waxed disc and Cellophane, or a screwtop or firm plastic top. Vinegar-based pickles must be secured by a firm plastic lid, or by a screwtop lined with a vinegar-proof disc. Paper alone is not good enough for pickles, which will dry out. Jars are best stored in a cool, dry, dark place.

Autumn Jam

1½lb/600g cooking apples
1½lb/600g ripe pears
1½lb/600g plums
1 teaspoon ground ginger
4lb/2kg sugar

Peel and core the apples and pears and cut them into pieces. Cut the plums in half and remove the stones. Put the fruit into the blender and blend until the apples and pears are finely chopped. Put into a saucepan and add the ginger. Simmer until the fruit is soft, adding a little water if necessary to prevent burning. Stir in the sugar until dissolved, and then boil quickly to setting point. Pour into warm jars and cover.

Blackcurrant Jam

2lb/1kg blackcurrants
½oz/15g butter
½ pint/250ml water
3lb/1.5kg sugar

Remove stems from the blackcurrants and rinse the fruit well. Grease a saucepan with the butter. Put the blackcurrants into the blender and blend until well broken up. Put into the saucepan. Rinse the blender with the water, and add the liquid to the pan. Bring the fruit to the boil and stir well until any fruit skins are soft. Add the sugar and stir over low heat until the sugar has dissolved. Boil rapidly for about 5 minutes until setting point is reached. Pour into warm jars and cover.

Gooseberry Jam

2lb/1kg gooseberries
½oz/15g butter
½ pint/250ml water
3lb/1.5kg sugar

Top and tail the gooseberries and rinse them well. Grease a saucepan with the butter. Put the gooseberries into the blender with the water and blend until well chopped. Put into the saucepan, bring to the boil, and simmer until the fruit skins are soft. Add the sugar and stir over a low heat until dissolved. Bring to the boil and boil rapidly for about 5 minutes until setting point is reached. Pour into warm jars and cover.

Pear Marmalade

6lb/3kg ripe pears
1 pint/500ml sweet cider
4lb/2kg sugar
Juice of 1 lemon

Wipe the pears and cut them in quarters without peeling. Remove the cores and cut the pears in pieces. Put into the blender, and chop coarsely. Bring the cider just to boiling point, add the pears, and simmer gently until the pear pieces are tender. Cool slightly, pour into the blender and blend until smooth. Return to the pan with the sugar and lemon juice and stir until the sugar has dissolved. Bring to the boil, and boil rapidly, stirring well, until setting point is reached. Pour into warm jars.

157

Rhubarb Conserve

4lb/1kg rhubarb
4lb/1kg sugar
1 lemon
2oz/50g blanched split
   almonds

Wipe the rhubarb and cut it into pieces. Put into the blender and blend until coarsely chopped. Put into a saucepan over low heat until the juice runs. Add the sugar, grated rind and juice of the lemon, and split almonds. Stir until the sugar has dissolved, and then boil for 45 minutes until thick and brown. Pour into warm jars and cover.

Apple Butter

1lb/400g cooking apples
¼ pint/125ml water
8oz/400g caster sugar
1 teaspoon ground cinnamon
¼ teaspoon ground allspice
½ teaspoon ground nutmeg
¼ teaspoon ground cloves
Pinch of salt
1 thin slice lemon

Use apples which become fluffy when cooked. Cut the apples into quarters, but do not peel them. Remove the cores, and then cut the flesh into pieces. Put all the ingredients into the blender and blend until the apples are finely chopped. Cook gently for 45 minutes, stirring occasionally, and pour into hot jars. The same recipe can be used for plums or damsons. This makes a good filling for tarts, but fruit butters used to be stored in wide-topped jars. They were then turned out, cut into slices, and served with cream.

Three Fruit Marmalade

1 grapefruit
1 sweet orange
2 lemons
3 pints/1.5 litres water
3lb/1.5kg sugar

Peel the grapefruit and scrape off all the white pith. Cut the fruit and peel into pieces. Cut the orange and lemons into pieces and take out the pips. Tie all the pips in a muslin bag. Chop the fruit and peel in small quantities in the blender, with some of the water. Mix with the remaining water and cook gently until the peel is soft and the mixture is reduced by half. The bag of pips should be suspended in the pan during this cooking, and then removed. Stir in the sugar over low heat until dissolved, and then boil rapidly to setting point. Test this by putting a spoonful on a cold saucer and leaving it for a minute or two. Push the mixture gently with a finger, and if it wrinkles, the marmalade has reached setting point. Cool slightly, stir and pour into warm jars. Cover with waxed discs, and put on lids when cold. This is a useful marmalade to make right through the year when bitter oranges are not available.

Opposite: Chunky Marmalade (page 161) and a selection of jams.

Chunky Marmalade

2lb/1kg Seville oranges
1 lemon
4 pints/2 litres water
4lb/2kg sugar

Cut the fruit in quarters and take out the pips. Tie the pips in a piece of muslin or thin linen. Put some of the fruit and some of the water into the blender. Cover and chop coarsely. Pour into a preserving pan, and continue the process until all the fruit has been chopped. Add remaining water, and tie the bag of pips to the handle so it floats in the mixture. Boil for 1 hour. Take out the bag of pips. Stir in the sugar over gentle heat until it has dissolved, and then boil to setting point, which should take about 20 minutes. Cool slightly and stir well, so that the peel is evenly distributed. Pour into warm jars, leave until cold, and cover.

Jelly Marmalade

8 Seville oranges
2 sweet oranges
2 lemons
8 pints/4 litres water
7lb/3.5kg sugar

Cut the oranges into four pieces without peeling. Remove the pips, put them into a piece of muslin or thin cotton and tie into a bag shape to suspend from the handle of the saucepan. Put some of the oranges and some of the water into the blender, and blend until the oranges are just chopped. Put into the pan. Continue blending the oranges and water until all the oranges are used up. Add remaining water, and leave to stand overnight. Boil for 30 minutes and strain through muslin or a jelly bag. Add the sugar together with the juice of the lemons. Heat gently and stir until the sugar has dissolved. Boil vigorously until the mixture 'jells' when tested on a cold plate. Remove any scum, and pour jelly into warm jars.

Fruit Mincemeat

4oz/100g suet
6oz/150g apples
8oz/200g raisins
8oz/200g currants
6oz/150g sultanas
4oz/100g mixed peel
2oz/50g blanched almonds
8oz/200g soft brown sugar
Juice and grated rind of 1 lemon
½ teaspoon ground mixed spice
½ teaspoon ground cinnamon
4fl.oz/100ml brandy or rum

If the suet is not already shredded, cut it into pieces. Peel and core the apples and cut into pieces. Put into the blender in small quantities together with the raisins, currants, sultanas and peel, and almonds. Chop finely and put into a bowl. Mix with the sugar, grated rind and lemon juice, spices, brandy or rum. Pack into clean dry jars and cover well. Store in a cool dry place.

Opposite: Chutneys and pickles (pages 162–5) add zest to cold meats, cheese and pies.

Cooked Mincemeat

¾ pint/375ml apple juice (see method)
6lb/3kg cooking apples
1lb/400g seedless raisins
1lb/400g currants
1lb/400g chopped mixed peel
1lb/400g shredded suet
1½lb/600g soft brown sugar
1 teaspoon ground mace
2 teaspoons ground cinnamon
3fl.oz/45ml brandy

The apple juice may be bought, but if plenty of apples are available, it can be made at home. Put 4lb/2kg apples through the mincing attachment, using the coarse screen. Put the pulp into a jelly bag or muslin and squeeze to get a clear juice. Put the juice in a large pan and bring to the boil. To make the mincemeat, peel the cooking apples and remove the cores. Cut the flesh into pieces and blend until the apples are chopped finely. Put the chopped apples into the saucepan of juice with the dried fruit, peel, suet, sugar and spices. Simmer slowly for 1 hour. Cool slightly, stir in the brandy, and put into screw-topped jars. This mincemeat will keep for 1 year.

Autumn Chutney

5lb/2.5kg apples
8oz/200g onions
8oz/200g stoned dates
4oz/100g sultanas
1 pint/500ml vinegar
1lb/400g Demerara sugar
½oz/15g ground ginger
½oz/15g salt

Peel and core the apples, and peel the onions. Cut them into chunks and put them into the blender in small quantities together with the dates. Grind until finely chopped. Put into a heavy pan with all the remaining ingredients, and bring to the boil. Simmer until brown and thick and pour into warm jars. Cover with lids fitted with vinegar-proof discs (honey jars are ideal, or jars that have contained pickles).

Date Chutney

1lb/400g stoned dates
4oz/100g onions
½ pint/250ml water
4oz/100g seedless raisins
½oz/15g garlic
6 chillies
4oz/100g sugar
1 teaspoon salt
1 pint/500ml vinegar

Block dates are the easiest and cheapest to use for this recipe. Cut the dates and onions in pieces and put into the blender with some of the water. Blend until they are well chopped. Put into a saucepan with the raisins and remaining water. Crush the garlic with a flat-bladed knife and also crush the chillies. Put the garlic and chillies into a piece of muslin or thin cotton and tie into a bag before hanging from the handle of the saucepan. Simmer the onion mixture until the onions are tender. Add the sugar, salt and vinegar and simmer for 30 minutes. Take out the bag of garlic and chillies. Blend the chutney for 30 seconds, and pour into warm jars.

Gooseberry Chutney

3lb/1.5kg gooseberries
½ pint/250ml vinegar
1¼lb/500g sugar
½oz/15g ground cloves

Top and tail the gooseberries and put them into the blender with some of the vinegar. Blend until chopped in small pieces. Put all the ingredients into a saucepan, bring to the boil, and simmer for 45 minutes, stirring until brown and thick. Pour into warm jars.

Indian Chutney

4 *large green peppers*
4 *large red peppers*
12 *green tomatoes*
3 *cucumbers*
2 *large onions*
1½oz/40g *salt*
8oz/200g *white-heart*
  cabbage
4oz/100g *sugar*
1¼ *pints/625ml cider vinegar*
1½oz/40g *mustard seed*
1 *teaspoon turmeric*
1 *teaspoon ground cinnamon*
2 *teaspoons ground ginger*
½ *teaspoon ground mace*
3 *bay leaves*

Remove the stems, membranes and seeds from the peppers. Put the peppers, tomatoes, unpeeled cucumbers and onions through the mincer attachment, using the coarse screen. Stir the salt into the vegetables and leave to stand overnight. Drain the vegetables through a colander, pressing down firmly to force out the brine which will have formed. Shred the cabbage finely with a shredding attachment, or through the fine screen of the mincer. Mix all the vegetables together and heat slowly to simmering point, stirring gently from time to time. Add the remaining ingredients and bring to boiling point. Boil for 3 minutes, and remove the bay leaves. Pour into hot jars and seal.

Orange Chutney

6 *medium oranges*
8oz/200g *onions*
1lb/400g *stoned dates*
1 *pint/500ml vinegar*
2 *teaspoons salt*
2 *teaspoons mixed spice*
2 *teaspoons ground ginger*

Choose thin-skinned oranges for this chutney. Cut the oranges in pieces, including the peel, and discard the pips. Peel the onions and cut into pieces. Put oranges, onions and dates into the blender in small quantities, and chop finely. Put all the ingredients into a heavy pan and cook together for 1¼ hours, stirring well until the mixture thickens. Pour into warm jars and cover with lids fitted with vinegar-proof discs.

Pear Chutney

4lb/2kg *pears*
2 *oranges*
1½lb/600g *sugar*
1 *teaspoon ground cloves*
1 *teaspoon ground cinnamon*
1 *teaspoon ground allspice*
1 *pint/500ml vinegar*
12oz/300g *seedless raisins*

Use ripe eating pears for this recipe. Peel the pears and core them, and cut the flesh into pieces. Put into the blender, and blend on low speed until chopped. Grate the rind from the oranges and squeeze out the juice from them. Put all the ingredients into a saucepan and bring to the boil. Simmer for 2 hours, stirring frequently, and pour into warm jars.

Plum Chutney

2lb/1kg stoned plums
1lb/400g carrots
1 pint/500ml vinegar
1lb/400g seedless raisins
1lb/400g soft brown sugar
1 garlic clove
1oz/25g chillies
1oz/25g ground ginger
1½oz/40g salt

Put the plums into the blender and blend on low speed until chopped, and put into a saucepan. Scrape or peel the carrots, according to age, and cut them into pieces. Put into the blender with some of the vinegar, and chop finely. Put into the saucepan with the rest of the vinegar, raisins and sugar. Crush the garlic clove with a flat-bladed knife, and chop the chillies. Add to the saucepan with the ginger and salt. Bring to the boil, and simmer until thick and brown, stirring well. Put into warm jars.

Rhubarb Chutney

2lb/1kg rhubarb
8oz/200g onions
1 pint/500ml vinegar
½oz/15g mustard seeds
1½lb/600g brown sugar
8oz/200g sultanas
¼ teaspoon Cayenne pepper
1 teaspoon mixed spice
1 teaspoon pepper
1 teaspoon ground ginger
1 teaspoon salt

Cut the rhubarb and onions in pieces. Put small quantities in the blender with a little of the vinegar. Cover and chop coarsely. When all the rhubarb and onions are chopped, put into a thick pan with all the other ingredients and simmer gently. Stir well until the sugar has been dissolved, and bring to the boil. Boil for 5 minutes, and then simmer until the mixture is thick and brown. Stir frequently. Put mixture into warm jars and cover well.

Green Tomato Chutney

1½lb/600g green tomatoes
1lb/400g apples
4oz/100g onions
1 pint/500ml vinegar
8oz/200g sugar
12oz/300g sultanas
1 teaspoon salt
1oz/25g ground mixed spice
Pinch of mustard powder

Cut the tomatoes and apples in pieces without peeling, and remove the cores. Peel the onions and cut into pieces. Put into the blender with some of the vinegar and chop finely. Put all the ingredients in a saucepan, bring to the boil, and then simmer for 1½ hours, stirring often, until thick and brown. Stir well, put into jars and cover.

Red Tomato Chutney

1lb/400g ripe tomatoes
4oz/100g apples
8oz/200g onions
1lb/400g seedless raisins
½ pint/250ml vinegar
4oz/100g soft brown sugar
1 teaspoon salt
1 teaspoon ground ginger
Pinch of Cayenne pepper

Dip the tomatoes into boiling water and remove the skins. Cut the tomatoes in pieces and remove the pips. Peel and core the apples and cut the flesh into pieces. Peel the onions and cut into pieces. Put the tomatoes, apples, onions and raisins into the blender with a little of the vinegar, and blend until finely chopped. Put all the ingredients into a saucepan, bring to the boil and simmer for 1 hour until thick and brown. Stir well and pour into warm jars.

Pepper and Onion Pickle

8 green peppers
3 large onions
4oz/100g sugar
12fl.oz/300ml vinegar
½oz/15g salt

Cut the peppers in quarters and remove the stems, membranes and seeds. Peel the onions and cut them in pieces. Put the peppers and onions into the blender in small quantities with just enough water to cover. Blend until vegetables are chopped in small pieces. Drain off the water and put the peppers and onions into a bowl. Cover with boiling water and leave for 15 minutes. Drain and cover again with boiling water, and leave for a further 15 minutes. Drain again and put into a large saucepan with the sugar, vinegar and salt. Bring to the boil and simmer for 30 minutes. Pack into hot preserving jars and seal. Use as a pickle, or add a few spoonfuls to winter casseroles or pies when peppers are expensive.

Cranberry Relish

1lb/400g cranberries
1 orange
3fl.oz/75ml boiling water
4oz/100g seedless raisins
1½lb/600g sugar
8oz/200g walnuts

Put the cranberries into ¼ pint/125ml cold water and boil until the skins break. Put into blender, cover, and blend for 5 seconds. Peel the orange and cut the flesh in small pieces. Add to the blender, cover and blend for 5 seconds. Add the cranberry and orange mixture to the boiling water, raisins and sugar. Bring to the boil and simmer for 20 minutes. Put the walnuts in the blender, cover, and chop coarsely. Stir into the cranberry mixture, cool and fill small jars. This may be eaten with turkey, pork or ham, and it is also very good as a filling for small tarts.

13 Saving Time and Money

It is obvious that the mixer, blender and other attachments save a great deal of time in the preparation of recipes. They can also save considerable time in preparing useful ingredients, such as chopping nuts, grating cheese or making breadcrumbs. This in turn can save money, when leftovers such as cheese and bread are processed and stored for later use in recipes. The blender is useful for converting leftovers into economical soups and pastes, which make the best of all sorts of odds-and-ends in the refrigerator. There is also great advantage to the keen cook, in being able to prepare flavoured butters, marzipan, praline and jam glazes quickly and cheaply, while the busy cook will be glad to be able to prepare baby food, invalid diets or health food herself, saving not only money but shopping time.

Breadcrumbs

Break bread into pieces about 1in/2.5cm square. Blend a little at a time, stopping the machine to scrape down. Empty out crumbs as they are made. Crumbs can vary from rough to powder texture, according to their intended use. Fresh bread should be processed in very small amounts. Stale bread will 'crumb' more easily, and bread can be crisped in the oven before blending to make crisp crumbs.

Biscuit Crumbs

Blend broken sweet biscuits on medium speed to make coarse or fine crumbs for flan cases, cheesecake bases, or uncooked biscuit-cakes.

Nuts

Blend a few nuts at a time, turning on and off at low speed until chopped as required.

Ice

Break ice roughly with a hammer (wrap it in cloth first), before putting into blender for crushing. Empty out as soon as broken up or ice will liquefy.

Herbs

Drop sprigs of fresh herbs on to cutters as they rotate. A little liquid aids easy blending.

Sugar

Granulated sugar can be put into the goblet, but do not fill it more than a quarter full. Blend at maximum speed for 30 seconds to produce caster sugar. Coloured sugar can be made for cakes and puddings if a few drops of food colouring are added during processing. The sugar should be stirred with a spatula once during blending to distribute colour.

Coffee

Put in just enough coffee beans to cover knives, or fill not more than one-third full. The blender can be timed to give coarse or fine grind.

Pulses and Rice

Lentils, split peas, rice, etc. can be treated like coffee beans. This cuts down cooking time if they are finely ground for soups.

Purée

Soft raw vegetables and fruit such as tomatoes and strawberries, or cooked fruits, need no extra liquid to become purée. The goblet should only be half full, and the mixture should be blended at high speed. Fruit need not be peeled before converting it into purée.

Dried Milk

Milk will be smooth if the water is put first into the goblet, then the dried milk powder. Blend for a few seconds at maximum speed.

Cream

Cream may be whipped by the blender, but will have greater volume if prepared with a mixer. Timing must be carefully watched and the blender must be stopped immediately the cream is thick. Keep turning the blender off and on rather than blending continuously.

Jams and Marmalade

The blender can chop such fruit as rhubarb, dried apricots and oranges for preserving, using the water to be included in the recipe. It will greatly speed cooking time.

Chocolate

Block chocolate should be broken up in small pieces and processed at low speed to required fineness. Not more than 3oz/75g should be chopped or grated at one time.

Sweets

Hard sweets such as peppermint rock or nut brittle can be crushed for use in puddings, ices and cakes. They should be blended at low speed in small amounts.

Candied Peel

Candied peel should be cut into 1in/2.5cm pieces, and fed gradually into the blender. Not more than 3oz/75g should be processed at one time. It is a good idea to blend the peel with a little icing sugar to prevent stickiness.

Fruit Juices

Canned and frozen juices taste fresh and delicious if blended for a few seconds at high speed, switching on and off once or twice during blending. Crushed ice can be added to the juices during blending.

Butter (Mixer)

About 1 pint/500ml cream is the smallest practical quantity to use, and it should be four days old. Put into mixing bowl, and using heavy beater, mix on low speed. Continue beating until butter comes into one lump. Switch off motor and drain buttermilk to use for cooking. Wash butter in cold water until water remains clear. Squeeze to extract water, salt to taste, and pat butter into shape.

Butter (Blender)

Blend cream on high speed for about 1 minute. Drain off buttermilk to use for cooking. Put clean cold water into blender with cream. Blend for 10 seconds, pour away water, and squeeze butter to extract water. Salt to taste, and pat butter into shape.

Cheese

Cut cheese into 1in/2.5cm cubes and feed gradually into the blender. Very hard cheese such as Parmesan should be cut in smaller pieces. As soon as the cheese becomes sticky, switch off, empty out cheese, and process another quantity. About 2oz/50g cheese should be processed in each batch. High speed for 6 seconds should be enough to grate most cheeses.

Children's Food

Food suitable for children can be blended into a smooth purée which is easily digested. A coarser texture can be produced for slightly older children. This means that meat, fish, poultry and vegetables from the ordinary family meal can be used for children; fruit and custard or milk pudding or cereal can be blended for a sweet course.

Dried milk for babies can be smoothly prepared in a blender which has been washed, rinsed and scalded before use. Powdered cereals can also be added to the milk in the blender. Flavoured milk drinks, or combinations of milk and eggs, or milk and fruit, will be popular with older children.

Diet Foods

For bland diets, or where an individual has to be fed, the blender can be used to make solid food into purée. A colander-and-sieve attachment is also useful for this type of food. Juicy fruits or vegetables require little or no extra liquid, but meat and fish can be made into a purée with milk, water, stock or egg. The blender should be started on low speed, and if the purée is thick it should be scraped·from the sides of the blender with the motor turned off before continuing processing.

Health Foods

A blender can be used to retain the complete goodness of fruit and vegetables for soups and drinks. Yogurt can be blended into drinks, and wheatgerm added for extra nourishment. If a juice-separator attachment is available, additional fruit and vegetable juices and extracts of herbs can be processed. Those who wish to avoid flour or fats will find that sauces and soups can be made without thickening with the aid of a blender.

Jam Glaze

A smooth jam glaze can be blended to use as a finish for flans, etc. Melt 4oz/100g apricot, strawberry, or raspberry jam, or redcurrant jelly with $\frac{1}{4}$ pint/125ml water. Boil for 4 minutes. Put into blender with 1 teaspoon/5ml lemon juice and blend until smooth. Sieve if necessary.

Leftovers

All kinds of leftover food can be used for a second meal after blending. Leftover meat, poultry or fish can be coarsely ground for use in loaves, mousses, soufflés and galantines. Small quantities of the same food can be blended into spreads and pastes. Vegetables, stock and gravy, can be blended into soups. Fruit can be made into a purée to blend with cream as a fool, or can be blended with custard or milk pudding to make a whip. Bread, biscuits, cakes, cheese, can all be blended to use as toppings, or as part of complete recipes.

Marzipan

A combination of mixer and blender makes marzipan of very fine texture. Blend 6oz/150g granulated sugar finely for 1 minute, using maximum speed. Mix with 6oz/150g icing sugar and 12oz/300g ground almonds, and using heavy beater on mixer at minimum speed, mix for 10 seconds. Add 1 egg and 2 teaspoons/10ml each of lemon juice and brandy, and increase speed slightly until a smooth paste is formed.

Pastry and Scone Mixes

To save time, make up large batches of pastry and scone mixes with heavy beater on mixer. Use flour and fat, but do not add water. Store 'crumb' mixture in polythene bag in a refrigerator. Weigh out and complete with milk or water as required.

Praline

Home-made praline is very useful for flavouring and decorating soufflés, creams and ices. Put together 3oz/75g caster sugar and 3oz/75g whole unblanched almonds in a thick saucepan, and set over low heat. Do not stir until sugar has melted and is turning in colour. Stir frequently until a good caramel, with the almonds well toasted. Turn on to an oiled tin. Break into pieces and blend on low speed until powdery. Keep in an airtight tin. Bought nut brittle and peppermint rock can also be blended in small amounts at low speeds to use for puddings, ices and cakes.

Index

Page numbers in *italic* refer to illustrations

Almond
  and Apricot Gateau 127
  Chocolate Biscuit Cake 129
  Flip 149
  Peach Pie 84
Anchovy Dip 141
  Spread 137
Apple
  and Walnut Salad 63
  and Walnut Stuffing 79
  Batter 91
  Butter 158
  Butterscotch Crumble 84
  Cake, Dorset 123
  Crunch 90
  Flummery 94
  Meringue 84
  Popovers 86
  Sauce 41, 43, 67
  Scones 116
  Snow 98
  Soup, Chilled 28
Applesauce Cake 124
Apricot
  and Almond Gateau 127
  flavouring 89
  Pork with Apple Sauce 41
  Stuffing 41, 77, 81
  Whip 95
Artichoke Soup 21
Asparagus Soufflé 56
  Soup 21, 51
Aubergine Dip 141
Aurora Sauce 69
Autumn Chutney 162
  Jam 157
Avocado Dip 140
  Soup, Chilled 29

Bacon
  and Cheese Spread 138
  and Cheese Toasts 139
  and Chicken Pâté 32
  and Liver Spread 137
  baked, in Apple Sauce 43
  Pâté 32
  Stuffing 80
Bakewell Pudding 85
Banana
  Flip 133, 148

Milk Shake, Chocolate 133, 148
  Mousse 96
  Nut Loaf 124
  Scones 116
Baps 108, 120
Barbecue Sauce 67
Basic Sour drink 154
Basic White Sauce 67
Batter(s)
  savoury 59
  Steak and Kidney 59
  sweet 91, 109–10
  to blend 16
  Yorkshire Pudding 58
Beef Fritters 60
Beef Olives 42
Beer Marinade 79
Beetroot Soup 21, 29
Biscuit(s)
  crumbs 15, 166
  doughs 13
  Honey 121
  mixer 113
  Tortoni 99
  Treacle 114
Blackcurrant Flummery 95
  Jam 157
Blender(s)
  attachments 9–10, 78
  batter 16
  breadmaking 106
  butter icing 130
  buttermaking 169
  cakemaking 106
  Cheese 41
  choosing 7–9
  cleaning 11
  fruit juices 168
  herbs 167
  ices 83
  leftovers 166, 170
  maintenance 11–12
  mayonnaise 73
  milk, dried 169
  quantities 15–16
  sauces 66
  soups 20
  speeds 15
  spreads 135

storing 11
  sugar 168
  technique 14–16
  types of 7–9, 25, 78, 134
Bloody Mary 155
Blue Cheese
  Dip 142
  Dressing 74
Bran Fruit Loaf 124
Brandy Butter 105
Bread(s)
  Baps 108, 120
  fancy 124
  Malt 108
  White 107, 117
  Wholemeal 107
Bread Sauce 68
Breadcrumbs 15, 166
Breadmaking 106–7, 117
Brown Bread Cream and Fruit
  Sauce 101
Brown Bread Ice Cream 98
Brown Sauce 68
Brown Sugar Brownies 125
Bun Dough 107
Buns
  Cornish Splits 115
  Mincemeat Pinwheel 109
Butter
  Apple 158
  Brandy 105
  Garlic 140
  Honey 139
  Honey Orange 140
  Icing 130
  Maple 139
  Parsley 140
  Peanut 140
  Rum 105
  Watercress 140
Buttermaking (Blender) 169
Buttermaking (Mixer) 169
Butters, flavoured 139–40
Butterscotch Sauce 105, 104

Cakemaking (Mixer) 18, 106
Cake(s)
  Almond and Apricot Gâteau
  127
  Apple Dorset 123

Applesauce 124
  Chocolate Almond Biscuit
  129
  Chocolate Bran 125
  Chocolate Brownies 125
  Chocolate Crumb 126
  Chocolate Macaroons 126
  Chocolate Meringues 126
  Chocolate Nut Gateau 128
  Chocolate Orange 129
  Chocolate Truffle 126
  Christmas Candle Ring 110
  Cinnamon Rolls 115
  Coffee Cake 127
  Dorset Apple 123
  Doughnuts 115
  Farmhouse Gingerbread 123
  Farmhouse Sponge 122
  fillings 132
  flavourings 121, 122, 128,
  130
  Gingerbread, Farmhouse
  123, 120
  Golden Pineapple 127
  Horseshoe Tea Ring 111
  Icebox 128
  Icings 130, 131, 132
  Lardy 109
  Light 116
  Macaroons, Chocolate 126
  Madeira 122
  Meringues, Chocolate 126
  Morning 123
  Nut Chocolate Gateau 128
  Orange Rock 129
  Pineapple, Golden 127
  Rock, Orange 129
  Sponges 121, 122, 120
  Stollen (batter) 109–10
  Truffle, Chocolate 126
  Victoria Sponge 121
Cakemaking (Mixer) 106
Caper Sauce 68
Caraway Cheese Spread 138
Carrot and Pineapple Cocktail
  147
Carrot and Tomato Soup 28
Celery Soup 22
Celery and Tomato Stuffing 80
Cheddar Dip, Hot 142

Cheese
  and Bacon Spread 138
  and Bacon Toasts 139
  and Mushroom Loaf 55
  and Onion Casserole 48
  and Tomato Spread 139
  blending 41
  Cream, Rolls 63
  Crumb Soufflé 58
  Dips 141, 142
  Mousse 53
  Pastry 112
  Pudding 63
  Rarebit Spread 139
  Sauce 68
  Soufflé 57
  Soup 22
  Spreads 138, 139
  to grate 170
Cheesecake(s)
  Baked 89, *119*
  bases 89–90
  Biscuit 89
  Brown Sugar 89
  Chocolate 90
  filling 90
  Walnut 90
Cherry Sauce 87
Cherry Soup, Chilled 29
Chestnut Cream, Chocolate
  94
Chestnut Soup 30
Chestnut Stuffing 81
Chicken
  and Bacon Pâté 32
  and Ham Loaf 50
  and Ham Pâté 33
  Honeyed Almond Roast 48
  in Curry Sauce 46
  Liver Herb Spread 136
  Liver Pâté 33, *52*
  Mousse 50
  Salad 54
  Savoury 45
  Sicilian 47
  Soufflé 57
  Spread 136
  Vol-au-vents 62

Children's Food, blended 169
Chocolate
  Almond Biscuit Cake 129
  Almond Pudding 93
  Banana Milk Shake *133*, 148
  Bran Cake 125
  Brownies 125
  Cheesecakes 90
  Chestnut Cream 94
  Cream Whip 149
  Crumb Cake 126
  Flavouring 89
  Fudge Sauce 101
  Ice Cream 98, 99
  Iced *133*, 150
  Macaroons 126
  Mexican 150
  Meringues 126
  Milk Shake, Banana *133*, 148
  Nut Gateau 128
  Orange Cake 129

Sauce 105
Syrup 146
to grate 168
Truffle Cakes 126
Chops, Braised 44
Choux Pastry 113
Christmas Candle Ring 110
Chutney *160*
  Autumn 162
  Date 162
  Gooseberry 162
  Indian 163
  Orange 163
  Pear 163
  Plum 164
  Rhubarb 164
  Sauce 69
  Tomato, Green 164
  Tomato, Red 165
Cider
  Lamb in 45, *77*
  Marinade 79
Cinnamon Rolls 115
Cocktail Dip 142
Coconut Pudding, Baked 88,
  103
Cod Cutlets, Stuffed 48
Cod in Tomato Sauce 46
Cod's Roe Pâté 37
Coffee
  Cake 127
  Cream Flan 92
  Cream Sauce 102
  Hot Foaming 153
  Ice cream 98
  Iced 150
  Walnut Mousse 96
Coleslaw 65
Confectioner's Custard 132
Corn Soup, Cream of 22
Corned Beef Pie 43
Corned Beef Spread 136
Cornish Splits 115
Cottage Griddle Scones 114
Coventry Tarts 86
Crab Soufflé 57
Cranberry Apple Sauce 72
  Relish 165
Cream Cheese Icing 131
Cream Cheese Rolls 63
Cream Crowdie 91
Cream maker 10
Cream soups 22, 23, 24
Cream to whip 169
Creaming butter and sugar 13
Creams, sweet
  Chocolate Chestnut 94
  for Puddings 93–4
  Marmalade 94
  Orange 94
  Wine 93
Croquettes, Meat 64
Crumbs
  Biscuit 166
  Bread 166
Crunchy Dip 141
Cucumber Mayonnaise 73
Cucumber Soup 30

Curdling, to remedy 18

Curry Dip 141Curry Sauce 46,
  69
Custard, Confectioner's 132
Custard Sauce 105

Daiquiri 152
Danish Soufflé 57
Date Whip 97
Devil Dressing 74
Devilled Egg Dip 143
  Ham Spread 136
  Sausages 63
Diet Foods, to blend 169–70
Dips
  Anchovy 141
  Aubergine 141
  Avocado 140
  Blue Cheese 142
  Cheddar, Hot 142
  Cheese 141, 142
  Cocktail 142
  Crunchy 141
  Curry 141
  Egg, Devilled 143
  Fish 141
  Horseradish 143
  Pickle 143
  Salad 144
  Seafood 144
  Tomato Yogurt 144
Dorset Apple Cake 123
Dough hook 10, 106
Doughnuts 115
Dressings
  Blue Cheese 74
  Devil 74
  Low-Calorie 75
  Salad 72, 74
  Sour Cream 75
  Yogurt Salad 75
Drinks
  Almond Flip 141
  Banana Chocolate Milk
    Shake *133*, 148
  Banana Flip *133*, 148
  Basic Sour 154
  blended *134*, 145–6
  Bloody Mary 155
  Carrot and Pineapple
    Cocktail 147
  Chocolate Banana Milk
    Shake *133*, 148
  Chocolate Cream Whip 149
  Chocolate, Iced,*133*, 150
  Chocolate, Mexican 150
  Chocolate Syrup 146
  Coffee, Hot Foaming 153
  Coffee, Iced 150
  Daiquiri 152
  Eggnog *133*, 155
  Eggnog, Honey 154
  Four Fruit Flip 150
  Fruit, Fresh, Shake *133*, 148
  Gin Fizz 144
  Ginger Peach 151
  Hawaiian Punch 151
  Honey Eggnog 154
  Honey Lemonade 151
  Ice Cream Soda 148
  Iced Chocolate *133*, 150

Iced Coffee 150
Lemon Cordial 152
Lemon and Orange Cup 152
Lemon Squash 152
Lemonade, Honey 151
Malted Milk Shake 149
Meal-in-a-Glass *133*,,147
Melon Strawberry Cooler
  150
Mexican Chocolate 150
Milk Shakes 148
Mint Cooler 151
Moscow Mule 153
Nursery Shake 149
Orange and Lemon Cup 152
Orangeade 152
Peach Ginger 151
Pineapple and Carrot
  Cocktail 147
Pineapple and Rum Shake
  154
Punch, Hawaiian 151
Punch, Winter Milk 153
Rum and Pineapple Shake
  154
Slimmers', Fresh Fruit Shake
  133, 148
Strawberry Melon Cooler
  150
Sugar Syrup 146
Tomato Cocktail 146
Tomato Juice 146
Tropical Shake 149
Vegetable Health Drink 147
Whisky Cooler 154
Winter Evergreen 153
Winter Milk Punch 153
Yogurt Shake 147
Drop Scones 116

Egg(s)
  blending 41
  Devilled Dip 143
  Eggnog, Honey 154
  Eggnog *133*, 155
  Eggnog, Honey 154
  Omelettes 55–6
  Pancakes 58, 83, *103*, *104*,
    116
  Sauce 68
  Soufflés 56–8
  Whites, to whisk 13, 17

Failures, to correct 17–19
Farmhouse Gingerbread *120*,
  123
Farmhouse Sponge 122
Fat, rubbing in 13, 113
Fillings
  Cake 132
  Cheesecake 90
  Flan 40
  Omelettes 55
  Pancakes, savoury 58
  Pastry 40
Fish dishes
  accompaniments 40
  Cakes 64
  Cod Cutlets, Stuffed 48

Cod in Tomato Sauce 46
Cod's Roe Pâté 37
Croquettes 64
Dips 141
Haddock Flan 62
Haddock Mousse 55
Haddock Pâté 38
Kipper Creams 60
Kipper Pâté 37
Mackerel, Baked Stuffed 49
Plaice Florentine 60
Plaice Stuffed 49
Puffs 58
Salmon Mousse 54
Salmon Pâté 39
Sardine Pâté 37
Seafood Pâté 38
Smoked Fish Pâté 38, 52
Soufflé 57
Soup 23
Spreads 137, 138
Flans, savoury 61, 62, 118
Fillings 40
Quiche Lorraine 61
Ratatouille 61
Smoked Haddock 62
Spanish Olive 61
Flans, sweet
Coffee Cream 92
Jam Glaze 171
Lemon 92
Lilian's Lemon 92, 104
pastry for 112
Flavourings
Cake 121, 122, 128
Cheese Dips 141
icings 130
soufflés, savoury 56–7
soufflés, sweet 88–9
Food processor 7, 9, 25
French Fritters with Cherry
  Sauce 87
Fritters
Beef 60
French 87
Fruited 87
Frosting, American 131
Fruit and Brown Bread Cream
  Sauce 101
Fruit flavouring 89
Fruit Flip 150
Fruit, Fresh, Shake 133, 148
Fruit juices, blending 169
Fruit Marmalade, Three 158
Fruit Mincemeat 161
Fruit Mousse 97
Fruit and Nut Ice Cream 100
Fruit Pancakes 83, 103
Fruit Purée 16
Fruit Soups 28, 29, 30
Fruited Fritters 87

Game Pâté 33
Gammon, Baked, with Apple
  Sauce 43
Garden Soup 23
Garlic Butter 140
Gazpacho Soup 30
Giblet Stuffing 76

Gin Fizz 144
Ginger Peach drink 151
Gingerbread, Farmhouse 123,
  120
Glacé Icing 130
Glaze, Jam 170
Golden Pineapple Cake 127
Golden Salad 65
Gooseberry Chutney 162
Gooseberry Jam 157
Green Mayonnaise 73
Green Goddess Mayonnaise
  73
Green Peppers, Stuffed 46

Haddock, Smoked, Flan 62
Haddock, Smoked, Mousse 55
Haddock, Smoked, Pâté 38
Ham and Chicken Loaf 50
Ham and Chicken Pâté 33
Ham Loaf 50
Ham, Devilled, Spread 136
Hawaiian Punch 151
Hazelnut Pâté 34
Health Foods, blending 170
Health Salad 65
Herb marinade 76
Herbs, to blend 167
Hollandaise Sauce 69
Honey
  and Walnut Scones 114
  Biscuits 121
  Butter 139
  Eggnog 154
  Lemonade 151
  Orange Butter 140
  Spice Pudding 86
Honeycomb Mould 91
Honeyed Almond Roast
  Chicken 48
Horseradish Cream 70
Horseradish Dip 143
Horseshoe Tea Ring 111

Ice, to crush 167
Ices
  Basic 98
  Brown Bread 98
  Chocolate 98, 99
  Coffee 98
  Fruit and Nut 100
  Lemon Water 99
  Milk 100, 133
  Nut 100
  Nut and Fruit 100
  Raspberry Honey 101
  Raspberry Water 99
  Soda 148
Icebox Cake 128
Iced Chocolate 133, 150
Iced Coffee 150
Icing, Mixer 13, 130
Icing
  American frosting 131
  Butter, Blender 130
  Butter, Mixer 130
  Cream Cheese 131
  Flavourings 130, 131
  Frosting, American 131

Glacé 130
Mocha Fudge 131
Royal 132
Indian Chutney 163
Indonesian Sauce 70

Jam
  Autumn 157
  Blackcurrant 157
  Glaze 170
  Gooseberry 157
Jelly Chiffon Pie 92
Jelly Marmalade 161
Jelly Whip 95, 104
Juice separator 10

Kidney Soup 23
Kidney and Steak Batter 59
Kipper Creams 60
Kipper Pâté 37
Kipper Spread 137
Kitchen centre 9, 78

Lafayette Mousse 96
Lamb
  in Cider 45, 77
  Pâté 34
  Roast, Pennywise 43
  Shoulder, Braised 44
Lamb's Liver Pâté 34
  with Apricot Stuffing 77
  with Mushroom Stuffing 77
Lamburgers 44
Lardy Cake 109
Leek and Potato Soup 24
Leftovers 7, 166, 170
Lemon
  and Orange Cup 152
  Cordial 152
  Crumb Pudding 85
  Flan, Lilian's 92, 104
  flavouring 89
  Flummery 95
  Sauce 105
  Squash 152
  Water Ice 99
Lemonade, Honey 151
Lentil Soup 24
Lentils, to grind 167
Light cakes 116
Lilian's Lemon Flan 92, 104
Liqueur flavouring 89
Liquids in blender 15
Liver
  and Bacon Spread 137
  and Pork Pâté 36
  Casserole 45
  Chicken Pâté 33, 52
  Chicken and Ham Spread 136
  Lamb's, Pâté 34
  Pâté, Quick 35
  Pâté, Rich 35
  Stuffed 49
Low-Calorie Dressing 75

Macaroons, Chocolate 126
Machines
  cleaning 11
  failures 17–19

maintenance 11–12
techniques 12–16
Mackerel, Baked, Stuffed 49
Madeira Cake 122
Magimix 9, 16, 25
Main courses 40–65
Malt Bread 108
Maltaise Sauce 69
Malted Milk Shake 149
Maple Butter 139
Marinades
  Beer 79
  Cider 79
  Herb 76
  Poultry 75
  Red meat 76
  Sweet and Sour 79
Marmalade
  Chunky 159, 161
  Cream 94
  Jelly 161
  Pear 157
  Three Fruit 158
Marzipan 13, 171
Mayonnaise
  blender 73
  Cucumber 73
  Green 73
  Green Goddess 73
  Mixer 73
  Tomato 73
Meal-in-a-Glass 133, 147
Meat accompaniments 40
Meat dishes
  Bacon and Chicken Pâté 32
  Balls 42
  Beef Fritters 60
  Beef Olives 42
  Chicken Liver Pâté 33, 52
  Chops, Braised 44
  Corned Beef Pie 43
  Croquettes 64
  Game Pâté 33
  Gammon, Baked 43
  Ham and Chicken Loaf 50
  Ham and Chicken Pâté 33
  Ham Loaf 50
  Lamb in Cider 45, 77
  Lamb's Liver Pâté 34
  Lamb Pâté 34
  Lamb Roast 43
  Lamb Shoulder 44
  Lamburgers 44
  Liver Casserole 45
  Liver Pâtés 34, 35, 36, 52
  Liver, Stuffed 49
  Pork with Apple Sauce 41
  Pork and Liver Pâté 36
  Pork Loaf 53
  Pork Sausages 64
  Pork, Sweet and Sour 42
  Pork Terrine 36
  Rabbit, Potted 36
  Rillettes 37
  Sausages, Devilled 63
  Sausages, Pork 64
  Shepherd's Pie 41
  Steak and Kidney Batter 59
  Tongue Mousse 54

Meat leftovers 40
Meat marinade 76
Meat Paste 135
Meat Spreads 136, 137, 138, 139
Melon Strawberry Cooler 150
Meringues, Chocolate 126
Mexican Chocolate 150
Milk, Dried, to blend 168
Milk Ice 100, *103*
Milk Shake 148
Milk Shake, Chocolate Banana *133*, 148
Mincemeat
  Cooked 162
  Fruit 161
Mincemeat Pinwheel Buns 109
Mint Cooler 151
Mint Sauce 70
Mixer(s)
  attachments 9–10, 11–12, *78*
  breadmaking 106–7
  butter icing 130
  butter-making 169
  choice of 7–8
  cleaning 11–12
  Kenwood Mini *78*
  maintenance 11
  mayonnaise 73
  pastry 111
  quantities 13
  speeds 13–14
  technique 12–13
Mocha Fudge Icing 131
Morning Cake 123
Moscow Mule 153
Mousseline Sauce 70
Mousses, savoury
  Cheese 53
  Chicken 50
  Haddock 55
  Salmon 54
  Tongue 54
Mousses, sweet
  Banana 96
  Coffee Walnut 96
  Fruit 97
  Lafayette 96
  Walnut, Coffee 96
Muffins 114, *120*
Mushroom and Cheese Loaf 55
Mushroom Sauces 68, 71
Mushroom Soufflé 57
Mushroom Soup 24
Mushroom Stuffing *77*, 81

Nursery Shake 149
Nut and Fruit Ice Cream 100
Nut Chocolate Gateau 128
Nut Ice Cream 100
Nut and Raisin Stuffing 76
Nuts, blending 168
Nutty Castles 87

Omelette
  Plain 55
  Soufflé 56
  Spanish 56

Onion
  and Cheese Casserole 48
  and Pepper Pickle 165
  Sauce 68
  Soup 24
Orange
  and Lemon Cup 152
  and Tomato Soup 30
  Cake, Chocolate 129
  Chutney 163
  Creams 94
  Rock Cakes 129
Orangeade 152

Pancakes, savoury 58
  Potato 116
Pancakes, sweet
  Fruit 83, *103*
  with Butterscotch Sauce *104*
Parsley Butter 140
Parsley Sauce 68
Paste, Meat 135
Pastes, blending 15
Pastry failures, to remedy 18
Pastry
  Cheese 112
  Choux 113
  Coventry Tarts 86
  fillings 40
  Mixer 13, 111
  Potato 113
  Rough Puff 112
  Shortcrust 112
  storing 171
  Sweet Flan 112
Pâté(s)
  Bacon (1) and (2) 32
  Chicken and Bacon 32
  Chicken and Ham 33
  Chicken Liver 33, *52*
  Cod's Roe 37
  Fish, Smoked 38, *52*
  Game 33
  Haddock, Smoked 38
  Hazelnut 34
  Kipper 37
  Lamb 34
  Lamb's Liver 34
  Liver 34, 35, 36
  Pigeon 35
  Pork and Liver 36
  Pork Terrine 36
  Rabbit, Potted 36
  Rillettes 37
  Salmon, Smoked 39
  Sardine 37
  Seafood 38
Pea Soup
  fresh 27
  Split 27
Peach Almond Pie 84
Peach Ginger 151
Peanut Butter 140
Pear Chutney 163
Pear Marmalade 157
Peas, split, to grind 167
Peel, candied, to chop 168
Pennywise Lamb Roast 43
Pepper and Onion Pickle 165

Pickle
  Dip 143
  Pepper and Onion 165
Pickles *160*, 165
Pies, savoury
  Corned Beef 43
  Shepherd's 41
Pies, sweet
  Jelly Chiffon 92
  Peach Almond 84
Pigeon Pâté 35
Pineapple
  and Carrot Cocktail 147
  and Rum Shake 154
  Cake, Golden 127
  Nut Vacherin 90
  Stuffing 80
Pizza 62
Plaice Florentine 60
Plaice, Stuffed 49
Plum Chutney 164
Pork
  and Liver Pâté 36
  in Apricot and Apple Sauce 41

  Loaf 53
  Sausages 64
  Sweet and Sour 42
  Terrine 36
Potato
  and Leek Soup 24
  Pancakes 116
  Pastry 113
  peeler attachment 10
  to mash 13
Poultry marinade 75
Poultry Stuffing 76
Praline 172
Prawn Stuffing 80
Prune Stuffing 81
Puddings, savoury
  Cheese 63
  Yorkshire 58
Puddings, sweet
  Apple Batter 91
  Apple Butterscotch Crumble 84
  Apple Crunch 90
  Apple Flummery 94
  Apple Meringue 84
  Apple Popovers 86
  Apple Snow 98
  Apricot Whip 95
  Bakewell 85
  Banana Mousse 96
  Biscuit Tortoni 99
  Blackcurrant Flummery 95
  Cheesecakes 89, 90
  Chocolate Almond 93
  Chocolate Cheesecakes 90
  Chocolate Chestnut Cream 94
  Coconut, Baked 88, *103*
  Coffee Cream Flan 92
  Coffee Walnut Mousse 96
  Coventry Tarts 86
  Cream Crowdie 91
  creams for 93–4

Date Whip 97
flans 92
flavourings 88–9
French Fritters with Cherry Sauce 87
Fruit Mousse 97
Fruit Pancakes 83, *103*
Fruited Fritters 87
Honey Spice 86
Honeycomb Mould 91
Jelly Chiffon Pie 92
Jelly Whip 95, *104*
Lafayette Mousse 96
Lemon Crumb 85
Lemon Flummery 95
Lilian's Lemon Flan 92
Marmalade Cream 94
Mousses 96–7
Nutty Castles 87
Orange Creams 94
Pancakes, Fruit 83, *103*
Peach Almond Pie 84
Pineapple Nut Vacherin 90
Queen of Puddings 85, *103*
Raisin 85
Raspberry Foam 91
Refrigerator Cake 93
sauces for 88–9, 101–1, 105
Speedy Pudding 88
Syllabub 97
Walnut Cheesecakes 90
Walnut Mousse, Coffee 96
Whips 95
Wine Cream 93
Zabaglione 97
Punch
  Hawaiian 151
  Winter Milk 153
Purées, blending 15–16, 167

Queen of Puddings 85, *103*
Quiche Lorraine 61

Rabbit, Potted 36
Raisin and Nut Stuffing 76
Raisin Pudding 85, *103*
Raspberry
  Foam 91
  Honey Ice 101
  Sauce 105
  Soup, Chilled 29
  Water Ice 99
Ratatouille Flan 61
Refrigerator Cake 93
Relish 165
Rhubarb Chutney 164
Rhubarb Conserve 158
Rice, to grind 167
Rillettes 37
Rock Cakes, Orange 129
Rough Puff Pastry 112
Royal Icing 13, 132
Rum butter 105
Rum and Pineapple Shake 154

Sage and Onion Stuffing 82
Salad Cream 72
Salad Dip 144
Salad Dressing 74

Salads
  Apple and Walnut 63
  Chicken 54
  Coleslaw 65
  Golden 65
  Health 65
  Walnut and Apple 63
Salmon
  Mousse 54
  Smoked, Pâté 39
  Spread 137
Sardine Pâté 37
Sardine Spread 138
Sauces, savoury
  Apple 67
  Aurora 69
  Barbecue 67
  Bread 68
  Brown 68
  Caper 68
  Cheese 68
  Chutney 69
  Cranberry Apple 72
  Curry 69
  Egg 68
  Hollandaise 69
  Horseradish Cream 70
  Indonesian 70
  Maltaise 69
  Mint 70
  Mousseline 70
  Mushroom 68, 72
  Onion 68
  Parsley 68
  Salad Cream 72
  Sweet Devil 72
  Sweet and Sour 71
  Tartare 74
  Tomato 46, 71
  Tomato Barbecue 72
  White 67
Sauces, sweet
  Brandy Butter 105
  Brown Bread Cream and
    Fruit 101
  Butterscotch 105
  Cherry 87
  Chocolate 105
  Chocolate Fudge 101
  Coffee Cream 102
  Custard 105
  Fruit and Brown Bread
    Cream 101
  Lemon 105
  Raspberry 105
  Rum Butter 105
  Sherry, Whipped 102
Sausage-filler attachment 9
Sausage Stuffing 82
Sausages, Devilled 63
Sausages, Pork 64
Savoury Florentine Layer 59
Savoury Chicken 45
Savoury Loaf, Hot 53
Scone mixture, to store 171
Scones 133

Apple 16
Banana 116
Cottage Griddle 114
Drop 116
Honey and Walnut 114
Walnut and Honey 114
Seafood
  Dip 144
  Pâté 38
  Soufflé 57
  Spread 138
Shepherd's Pie 41
Sherry Sauce 102
Shortcrust Pastry 112
Sicilian Chicken 47
Smoked Fish Pâté 38
Soufflé, Cheese Crumb 58
SouffléOmelette 56
Soufflés, savoury 56–7
Soufflés, sweet 88–9
Soup(s)
  Apple, Chilled 28
  Artichoke 21
  Asparagus 21
  Avocado, Chilled 29
  Beetroot 21
  Beetroot, Chilled 29
  Blending 15, 20, 134
  Carrot and Tomato 28
  Celery 22
  Cheese 22
  Cherry, Chilled 29
  Chestnut 30
  Corn, Cream of 22
  Cucumber, Chilled 30
  Fish, Creamed 23
  Garden 23
  Gazpacho 30
  Kidney 23
  Leek and Potato 24
  Lentil 24
  Mushroom 24
  Onion, Cream of 24
  Orange and Tomato 30
  Pea, fresh 27
  Pea, split 27
  Potato and Leek 24
  Raspberry, Chilled 29
  Tomato 27
  Tomato and Carrot 28
  Tomato and Orange 30
  Tomato and Potato 28
  Vichyssoise 24, 26
  Watercress 28
Sour Cream Dressing 75
Spanish Olive Flan 61
Spanish Omelette 56
Speedy Pudding 88
Sponge Cakes 120, 121, 122
  Drops 122
  Farmhouse 122
Spreads
  Anchovy 137
  Bacon and Cheese 138
  Bacon and Cheese Toasts 139
  Bacon and Liver 137

blending 15
Butters 139–40
  Caraway Cheese 138
  Cheese and Bacon 138
  Cheese and Bacon Toasts 139
  Cheese and Tomato 139
  Cheese Rarebit 139
  Chicken 136
  Chicken Liver Herb 136
  Corned Beef 136
  Devilled Ham 136
  Fish 137, 138
  Garlic Butter 140
  Ham, Devilled 136
  Honey Butter 139
  Honey Orange Butter 140
  Kipper 137
  Liver and Bacon 137
  Maple Butter 139
  Meat 136, 137, 138, 139
  Orange Butter, Honey 140
  Parsley Butter 140
  Peanut Butter 140
  Salmon 137
  Sardine 138
  Seafood 138
  Tomato and Cheese 139
  Watercress Butter 140
Steak and Kidney Batter 59
Stollen (batter) 109–10
Strawberry Melon Cooler
  150
Stuffed Cod Cutlets 48
Stuffed Green Peppers 46
Stuffed Liver 49
Stuffed Plaice 49
Stuffed Tomatoes 47
Stuffings
  Apple and Walnut 79
  Apricot 41, 77, 81
  Bacon 80
  Celery and Tomato 80
  Chestnut 81
  Giblet 76
  Mushroom 77, 81
  Nut and Raisin 76
  Pineapple 80
  Poultry 76
  Prawn 80
  Prune 81
  Raisin and Nut 76
  Sage and Onion 82
  Sausage 82
  Tomato and Celery 80
  Walnut and Apple 79
Sunbeam
  blender 134
  kitchen centre 9, 78
Sweet Devil Sauce 72
Sweet Flan Pastry 112
Sweet and Sour Marinade 79
Sweet and Sour Pork 42
Sweet and Sour Sauce 71
Sweets, to chop 168
Syllabub 97
Syrups 146

Tartare Sauce 74
Temperatures 6
Terrine of Pork 36
Tomato
  and Carrot Soup 28
  and Celery Stuffing 80
  and Cheese Spread 139
  and Orange Soup, Chilled 30
  and Potato Soup 8
  Barbecue Sauce 72
  Chutney, Green 164
  Chutney, Red 165
  Cocktail 146
  Juice 146
  Mayonnaise 73
  Sauce 46, 71
  Soufflé 57
  Soup 27
  Yogurt Dip 144
Tomatoes, Stuffed 47
Tongue Mousse 54
Treacle Biscuits 114
Tropical Shake 149
Truffle Cakes, Chocolate 126

Vegetable Health Drink 147
Vegetables, blending 15
Vichyssoise Soup 24, 26
Victoria Sponge 121
Vol-au-vents, Chicken 62

Walnut
  and Apple Salad 63
  and Apple Stuffing 79
  and Honey Scones 114
  Cheesecakes 90
  Coffee Mousse 96
  Loaf 124
Watercress Butter 140
Watercress Soup 28
Whipped Sherry Sauce 102
Whips
  Apricot 95
  Chocolate Cream 149
  Date 97
  Jelly 95, 119
Whisky Cooler 154
Whisking failure, to remedy
  17
White Sauce 67
Wholemeal Bread 107
Wine Cream 93
Winter Evergreen 153
Winter Milk Punch 153

Yeast cookery 106
Yeast Dough (Mixer) 13
Yogurt Salad Dressing 75
Yogurt Shake 147
Yogurt Tomato Dip 144
Yorkshire Pudding 58

Zabaglione 97